Letts go to
Portugal

by Harold Dennis-Jones

First published 1974   Completely revised 1977
by Charles Letts and Company Limited
Diary House, Borough Road, London, SE1 1DW
Designed by Ed Perera
Cover: Braga, photograph: Portuguese National Tourist Office
Photographs: Harold Dennis-Jones, p. 48
        A. F. Kersting, London, pp. 28, 38
        Portuguese National Tourist Office, pp. 37, 47, 58, 67
Illustrations: Ed Perera, pp. 16, 55
© Text: Harold Dennis-Jones
Standard Book Number 85097 106 3
Printed in Great Britain by
Letts Erskine Limited, Dalkeith

Contents

Facts at your Fingertips

Passports and Visas

To travel to Portugal you need either a valid full passport (blue cover) or a valid British Visitor's Passport (pink). The former is valid world-wide for 10 years and costs £8. The latter can be used only for Portugal and certain West European countries (including those you are likely to travel through on surface routes to Portugal): it lasts 1 year and costs £4.

To get a full passport you must apply to the right Passport Office for the address where you live: this is clearly shown on the application forms which you can obtain from any Passport Office, Principal Post Office, or travel agent. You need 2 passport photographs: identical full-face pictures from automatic machines are accepted. One of these and your application form must be signed by someone in a specific position, such as your bank manager, a solicitor, Justice of the Peace, and so on, who has known you personally for at least 2 years. Birth certificates, marriage certificates for married women, are needed for first applications. Send in completed applications as early as possible, and at least 3 weeks before your departure date. Genuinely urgent applications are dealt with in hours by Passport Offices.

A British Visitor's Passport is obtained immediately by personal application at any Principal Post Office. 2 passport photographs, and proof of identity—birth certificate or National Health card, are needed.

Visas for Portugal are not needed for citizens of the UK, USA, or most European countries, but may be required by certain Commonwealth and other nationals. Information can be obtained at any Portuguese consulate or the National Tourist Office (see p. 19): also from most travel agents, though their information is not always up-to-date. If your stay lasts more than 90 days you must register with the Portuguese police.

Personal Insurance

Before setting out for Portugal it is worth seeing that you are insured against all the extra costs you may incur as a result of accident or illness—doctor's and hospital fees (there is no National Health Insurance and charges can be extremely high), additional hotels, special flights home, and so on. Insurance costs very little and can be obtained through Lloyd's, Europ Assistance, the motoring organisations, the Caravan Club, and many other organisations. 'Holiday travel' policies cover you also against loss of deposits if you have to cancel at the last moment. The advan-

tage of the scheme run by Europ Assistance (which can also
include cover for loss or theft of baggage or money) is that the
company gives immediate guarantee of payment to doctors,
hospitals, hotels, and so on.

Addresses:
RAC, 83 Pall Mall, London SW1Y 5HL
AA, PO Box 50, Basingstoke, Hants RG21 2ED
Europ Assistance, 269-273 High Street, Croydon, Surrey CR0 1QH
Caravan Club, East Grinstead House, East Grinstead, West Sussex
   RH19 1VA
Camping Club of Great Britain, 11 Lower Grosvenor Place,
   London SW1W 0EY

Health Regulations

Health certificates and vaccinations are not required by visitors
from Europe or the USA unless there has been an outbreak of
smallpox or some similarly dangerous infectious disease in the area
where they live or are travelling through.

Customs

Portuguese Customs concessions follow the same general lines as
those of other European countries. You can take in all personal
effects, including clothing, toilet articles, and jewellery, without
paying duty. You can also take in 250 g (about 9 oz) of tobacco
or tobacco goods (i.e. 200 cigarettes, or 100 cigarillos, or 50
cigars), small quantities of toilet water or perfume for personal
use, one bottle of wine, but only half a bottle of spirits. Sports
equipment, camping gear, a child's pushchair, binoculars, a radio,
tape recorder, musical instruments, and portable typewriter are
allowed in without quibble. Professional photographers and keen
amateurs should however note that, strictly speaking, only one
camera and 5 rolls of unexposed film, and only one cine camera
with 2 reels of film, may be carried into Portugal. In practice
questions are rarely asked about cameras. Reasonable quantities
of foodstuffs are allowed. Non-commercial gifts to the value of
2500 escudos (just under £45) may also be imported.

On their return to Britain, UK residents aged 17 or over may
import the following goods free of tax and duty if bought in an
airport or ferry duty-free shop, or in a non-Common Market
country such as Portugal:

250 g of tobacco goods (about 9 oz of pipe tobacco, 200 large
cigarettes or 100 cigarillos, or 50 cigars);

1 litre ($1\frac{1}{3}$ ordinary bottles) of strong spirits (such as whisky,
brandy, and most liqueurs) **or**

2 litres (2⅔ ordinary bottles) of weak spirits (such as advocaat, or fruit liqueurs), fortified wine (port, vermouth, for instance), or sparkling wine;
2 litres (2⅔ ordinary bottles) of still table wine.

UK residents of any age may also import from duty-free shops or non-Common Market countries:
50 g (2 fluid oz) of perfume
¼ litre (9 fluid oz) of toilet water
£10 worth of other goods (keep receipts).

If you have bought the goods in an ordinary shop (that is, paid the ordinary duty and tax) in France or another Common Market country on your way back from Portugal, and are returning direct from one of those countries, the above allowances are raised to:
400 g of tobacco goods (14 oz, or 300 cigarettes, or 150 cigarillos);
1½ litres of strong spirits **or**
3 litres of weak spirits, fortified or sparkling wine;
3 litres of still table wine;
75 gm (3 fluid oz) of perfume;
⅜ litre (13 fluid oz) of toilet water;
£50 worth of other goods (keep receipts).

If purchases from Common Market and non-Common Market countries are mixed, the lower allowances apply.

Currency

The easiest way of taking money to Portugal is to buy sterling traveller's cheques from any bank (take your passport). However, in view of continuous currency fluctuations, you may find it worth while buying traveller's cheques in other denominations, such as West German marks, Swiss francs, and so on. You can take as much money in and out of Portugal as you wish, but you must not leave Britain with more than £25 in British banknotes.

The Portuguese currency unit is the escudo (abbreviated $) and the rate of exchange at the time this book goes to press is around 58$ to the £ sterling and 33$ to the US $1. The escudo is divided into 100 centavos. Note the normal way of writing prices: '1$50' means 1 escudo 50 centavos. '25$' means 25 escudos. But $25 means 25 centavos.

Coins and notes. Nickel-coloured—2½, and 5, and 10 escudos. Copper-coloured—10 and 50 centavos and 1 escudo. At the time of writing the existence of other coins seems purely theoretical. In fact, small change in particular is often so scarce in Portugal that it is worth getting as much as possible immediately after arrival and seeing that the stock is continuously topped up. Even so, shopkeepers are sometimes reduced to giving boxes of matches and other tiny items as change in place of small coins. Banknote denominations are: 20, 50, 100, 500, and 1,000 escudos.

Escudos-sterling equivalents at 58$=£1

$	$50	1$	2$50	5$	10$	25$	50$	100$
£p	1p	2p	4½p	9p	17p	43p	86p	£1·72

Sterling-escudos equivalents at £1=58$.

£p	1p	5p	10p	25p	50p	£1
$	0$58	2$90	5$80	14$50	29$00	58$00

Sterling and dollar notes and traveller's cheques can be changed at most banks, some travel agents, hotels (provided you are staying there), the Rossio Station in Lisbon, and at special exchange offices (cambios). Bank procedures are apt to be long-winded outside main tourist regions: use the exchange offices if possible; these also have longer opening hours—one or two in Lisbon may even stay open all night. Take your passport when changing money.

Bank opening times. Bank hours are 9.30-12.00 and 14.00-16.00., Sats 9.30-11.30. All banks close on Sundays and public holidays.

Climate

Thanks to the Gulf Stream and the nearness of the Atlantic, Portugal has a generally mild climate, even in the country's cooler northern half. In the south, along both the west-facing and south-facing coasts the climate is Mediterranean—that is, with dry warm summers and mild winters—despite the fact that these shores face the Atlantic. Rain, sometimes heavy and prolonged, falls mainly between November and February. Spring comes early, especially in the south. Summers are distinctly hot by British standards, but not unpleasantly so. Among the inland northern hills and on the high Serra da Estrela, winter is, of course, colder than on the coast, and in the south occasional high winds are possible in summer, even when the weather is completely dry. Most British visitors find the Portuguese climate extremely pleasant.

Clothing Leisure clothes can be worn all the time on the Algarve coast. In Lisbon and the more expensive hotels in Oporto, Cascais, Estoril, and similar places, formal suits and dresses should be taken for the evenings. The Portuguese are still inclined to be rather proper. While no rules are laid down, they prefer visitors to wear 'modest' clothing when visiting churches—trousers, not shorts, for men and not over-skimpy clothes for women.

Average Monthly Temperatures in Centigrade and Fahrenheit.

	Max	Min		Max	Min
Jan	15/59	7/45	July	28/82	18/64
Feb	15/59	9/48	Aug	28/82	17/63
Mar	16/61	9/48	Sept	25/77	16/61
Apr	18/64	10/50	Oct	24/75	16/61
May	22/71	13/55	Nov	19/66	12/54
Jun	25/77	15/59	Dec	15/59	9/48

Time

Portugal keeps Central European time—1 hour ahead of the UK in winter, but the same in summer. (Summer Time extends from the first Sunday in May to the first Sunday in September, after the autumnal equinox.)

Getting There

Air Services

British Airways (BA for short) and Portuguese Airways (TAP) both operate direct flights daily from London (Heathrow) to Lisbon. In the summer one or other airline flies direct to Faro every day and there are also fairly frequent flights to Oporto. Some British Caledonian (BCAL) and Varig flights to South America also put down at Lisbon. Fares to Lisbon at the time of going to press are: £118.50 1st-class and £75 economy single, £118.50 one-month excursion by day flights, £99.50 by night. To Faro you pay £119.50 1st-class, £85 economy single, and £127 for one-month excursion returns by day flights, £106.50 by night via Lisbon. With excursion tickets you must not break your journey, nor can you start your return until the sixth day after arrival.

By Rail

The rail-and-boat overland journey to Lisbon takes 38 to 43 hours. A change is necessary at Paris, and also at Irun, on the French-Spanish frontier, unless you travel by the Puerta del Sol (Sun

Gate) express between Paris and Madrid or the through train via Valladolid to Lisbon. For the Puerta del Sol you pay an inclusive charge covering 1st or 2nd-class sleeper or 2nd-class couchette, dinner, and breakfast. The rate is not high. From Madrid fast expresses are available to Lisbon. The Sud Express (Paris-Irun) connects at Irun with fast through-trains to Lisbon and Oporto. Basic return fares, London-Lisbon, liable to variations because of exchange fluctuations, range from about £98 to £105 1st-class and £80 to £85 2nd-class. A booklet giving full information about travel by train and cross-channel boat is available free from British Rail.

By Sea
Passengers without cars can travel to Lisbon by P. & O. and other freight and passenger lines. Sailing dates are irregular, and passages usually need to be booked months in advance. Consult a reliable travel agent. Whether or not you have a car you can travel by:
Ferry routes to Bilbao and Santander: To Bilbao (Swedish Lloyd)-passengers £21-£68 according to cabin, cars from free to £20 according to number of passengers. To Santander—passengers £23-£80, cars from free to £40.
Short Channel crossings: passengers £6.60 each way, cars under 14′ £12-£17.
Southampton-Le Havre or Cherbourg: passengers £9, cars £17-£21.

Inclusive Holidays
Some travel firms provide inclusive-price holidays in Portugal. We have divided them into major categories and added notes where necessary. All tour operators mentioned are located in London, unless otherwise indicated.

Beach-and-sun holidays include air travel by charter or scheduled flights, accommodation, and in most cases full board, though half board (breakfast and one main meal), or simply bed and breakfast may sometimes be offered instead. The resorts used are mostly on the Algarve coast or the Costa do Sol, though other popular resorts such as Figueira da Foz, Espinho, and so on, are also sometimes included, together with one or two places still little known. Lists and brochures of the travel firms offering these holidays can be obtained from any travel agent—they are too numerous to give details here.

A number of firms—Thomson, Travel Club, and others—offer cheap short winter holidays.

Villa Holidays include the rental of a villa or apartment, together with maid service as specified. Air travel by either charter or scheduled flight can be included if you wish, or the firm will make

bookings for your car and your party on any ferries you choose
and sometimes also reserve hotels en route. Or you can do all this
for yourself.

Algarve Agency (specialise in the more comfortable villas and
apartments and are chief—sometimes sole—agents for some of the
Algarve's most luxurious developments), Algarve Villas, Beach
Villas (Cambridge), Continental Villas, Holiday Villas, Meon
Travel (Petersfield), Owner's Services Ltd. (Broxbourne), Palmer &
Parker, Starvillas, Sun Villas, Travel Club (Upminster), Villas
Portuguesas.

Motoring Holidays These are of two types—either a complete tour
is booked for you including ferry crossings, overnight hotels en
route, and hotel and full board at the destination resort; or you
buy fly-drive arrangement that includes basically only air travel
and car hire for a specified period, with pre-reserved hotel
accommodation as a possible optional extra.

British Airways Fly-Drive and Freewheeler Holidays, at the West
London Air Terminal, (under Freewheeler arrangements 2 or more
people travelling together get a car free for 7 days for the price of
normal return fares) operate these holidays, together with Cook's
Motoring Holidays, Lane's Travel Service, and TAP (Portuguese
Airlines).

British Airways and other airlines will also arrange to have a hire
car waiting at your destination airport. In addition, several villa
holiday firms can offer fly-drive arrangements in combination with
villa rental and almost all will book cars on your behalf for use
after arrival adding the cost to the one bill.

Special interest and unusual holidays
Birdwatching: Academy Travel, and Gold Bond.
Tours of Portugal: Inter-Church Travel, Meliá Travel, St
Christopher Tours, Trafalgar Travel, Wings, and International
Caravan Holidays (caravan tours).
Cruises: Shaw Savill, P & O Ferries, etc.
Golf: Global, Travel Club (Upminster), John Morgan, and others.

Internal Transport

Portugal has a well-developed transport system, with two domestic
air routes from Lisbon, trains serving all the main areas, and buses
and long-distance coaches reaching even the smallest villages
though not necessarily quickly or frequently. Trams and/or buses
and, in Oporto, trolleybuses operate in the towns. Taxis are
readily available in towns and resorts.

Domestic Air Services. Lisbon-Oporto and Lisbon-Faro: 2 services
daily each, costing 1380$ and 1340$ respectively.

Trains Main lines run from Lisbon northward to Coimbra, Aveiro and Oporto; south to the Algarve; and east and north-east to the Spanish frontier at Marvão and Vilar Formoso. International expresses to Madrid and Irun run on the last two routes. Branch lines reach to various parts of the interior. Long-distance trains are hauled by diesel locomotives and are comfortable.

In addition there are electric short-distance services from Lisbon (Rossio) to Sintra and the north, and from Lisbon (Cais do Sodre) to Estoril and Cascais. Trains for the Algarve and the south start from Barreiro Station, south of the Tagus. You reach it by the Sul e Sueste ferries that start from beside Lisbon's 'Black Horse Square' (Praça do Comercio).

Trains have first and second-class coaches. Fares are 0$70 and 0$50 per km. Supplements are charged on fast trains and seats should be reserved in advance for long journeys (10$). Children under 12 pay half fares.

Coaches Services between main towns are comfortable and provide a very good way of seeing the country. Fares are mostly in the region of 0$60 to 0$70 per km.

Town buses, trams, and trolleybuses Vehicles are comfortable and services reasonably frequent; British-built double-deckers operate in Lisbon, and trams, buses, and trolleybuses in Oporto. Fares vary slightly according to distance: the maximum is 4$. Lisbon boasts a fairly modern underground system. The charge per journey is 3$50.

Boats and ferries Passenger services are all cheap. The 1-hour journey from Peniche to Berlenga Island, for instance, costs about 40$ return.

Taxis Portuguese taxis are efficient and usually quite comfortable. Prices vary somewhat from region to region but are usually around 8-10$ for the first km and 4$ per km after that. For six-seater vehicles prices are a little higher, but there is no extra night charge. Prices for regular journeys—for instance, from town centre to airport or outlying hotel—are officially fixed and there is no need to bargain or worry. Get into taxis from the pavement side. Entering from the road side makes you liable to an on-the-spot fine.

Accommodation

Hotel-type accommodation in Portugal is normally dependable and attractive. But prices have risen in recent years and the pound sterling has been sinking so that hotels are no longer notably cheap.

All accommodation is officially inspected and graded.

Five types of establishment are recognised: hotels (*hoteis*), *pousadas, albergarias, pensões, estalagens,* and motels. The different types are distinguished chiefly by their public rooms and by the services they offer.

Hotels are divided into 5 classes, with one to five stars. One-star establishments are simple, and relatively few rooms have private baths or showers. In the two-star category every bedroom has a private bath or shower; and above that all rooms have private baths.

The pousadas are State-run inns, strategically located to serve motor tourists. They vary in size and type. Some occupy modern buildings: others are housed in beautifully-modernised ancient palaces and convents, such as those at Estremoz, Evora, and Obidos. One or two are fairly simple, but all are elegantly furnished with typical local handicraft-work. Prices are reasonably low. Between June 1st and October 31st your maximum stay is limited to 5 days. From November 1st to May 31st there is no limit to how long you stay in pousadas with over 10 rooms, but you cannot stay more than 7 days in those with 5-10 rooms and 5 days in those with under 5 rooms. Very early booking is absolutely essential—and well worth the effort if you want a thoroughly enjoyable tour of the country.

Estalagens, divided into five and four-star categories, are privately owned inns that fill roughly the same needs as the pousadas.

Guesthouses (*pensões:* sing. *pensão*) are awarded one to four stars according to their standards. Those with four stars normally have every room with private bath: three-star establishments have a high proportion of private baths. Public rooms and services, naturally, are simpler than hotels. The title *albergaria* is given to specially comfortable four-star pensões. While many of these guesthouses are extremely simple their service is always willing and they provide very good value for money. Many occupy only the upper floors of modern buildings.

Motels are given either three or two stars and are not very numerous. They serve fairly strictly as overnight stopping-places for motorists. Their facilities do not include restaurants, though they serve breakfasts.

Rooms without bath, where available, are naturally cheaper.

All hotels and other types of accommodation add 10% for service, and in resorts a further 3% 'resort tax' is added. 30% is deducted for single occupancy of a double room, and all prices of coastal resort hotels are reduced by 15% from November to February inclusive. Children under 8 are everywhere entitled to a 50%

discount on meals. You pay 35% of the normal price for an extra bed in the room.

Prices depend on a lot more than just the official classifications, so that it is impossible to quote exact rates. Here are some rough indications of the prices you can expect to pay:

Accommodation	Room for 2 persons		Breakfast	Main Meal
	With private bath	Without bath		
Hotels	(in escudos)			
*****	600–1400		40–45	200–350
****	380– 500		28–40	125–250
***	280– 360		25–35	90–185
**	150– 275	110–150	14–20	75–150
*	120– 195	100–185	11–16	70–125
Albergarias				
****	200– 345		20–26	80–150
Pensões				
****	150– 250		15–25	90–200
***	120– 220		10–20	70–120
**	110– 160	70–100	9–15	60–100
*		60– 90	8–12	40– 80
Estalagens				
*****	280– 465		20–29	120–205
****	100– 295		15–29	80–140
Pousadas	135– 180	85	20–25	80–135
(rooms at 2 or 3 de luxe pousadas cost the same as better class hotels)				
Motels				
****	260– 400		23–29	—
***	200– 320		20–25	—

Electricity is mostly 220 volts AC. Do not rely on the less expensive hotels having electric razor sockets.

Laundry and dry cleaning is looked after efficiently by most hotels, though you will find no shortage of laundries (*lavandarias*) and dry cleaners (*limpezias*) in even small towns. Prices are not high.

Villas and apartments Large numbers of villas and apartments are available for letting in or near all the main Algarve coast resorts. In standard they vary from the merely comfortable to the thoroughly luxurious, and prices tend to be fairly high—though not frighteningly so. It may sometimes be possible to arrange the let at somewhat lower rates through an office in Portugal but it is very much easier to rent through British-based companies. If you pay more it is because you get the services of on-the-spot British staff as well as a reasonable assurance that the accommodation satisfies British standards.

Letting prices are quoted either inclusive of air transport and transfers between Faro airport and the villa, or for accommodation only, in which case you make all your own travel arrangements. Maid service for specified times—often six days a week—is normally included.

Buying Property Large numbers of villas and apartments are being offered for sale in the Algarve for investment, retirement, and holiday use. Most of the firms involved are well-known and thoroughly reputable. Some are London-based or have London offices. Others can best be contacted by visiting the Algarve and picking up a copy (for instance, in the Faro Turismo office) of a publication such as What's On in the Algarve, where both local and international firms advertise. It is as well, in any case, to get to know the region before deciding on a purchase.

Youth Hostels There are about 15 hostels only, situated at strategic points. Some are open only in summer, and may cater for only males or only females. Overnights cost 25$, if you are under 30, 50$ for older members. Continental breakfast, when available, costs 12$50; main meal 25$. Standards are acceptable, though a little lower perhaps than in the best British hostels. Further information can be obtained from the YHA, 29 John Adam Street, London WC2.

Restaurants

All Portuguese restaurants are officially inspected and graded into four classes—de luxe, first, second, and third. They are compelled by law to display menus and prices outside the establishments. Towns and tourist resorts usually offer a good choice of eating places. However they are less frequent in smaller spots. In case of need, all hotels, *pousadas, estalagens* and motels welcome non-residents. If you are using them, note that their mealtimes are usually 12.00 or 12.30 to 14.00 or 14.30, and 19.30 or 20.00 to 21.00 or 23.00 (later in big towns). Breakfast is normally served from 8.00 on, rarely earlier.

Almost without exception, restaurants are attractive and well run and provide very good value for money—even though prices in the Algarve, in particular, are well above what you pay in places less filled with foreign visitors. Many restaurants serve fixed-price table d'hôte meals that may include up to six courses.

Prices vary considerably. Off the beaten track you can eat surprisingly well for 90-110$, including 3 courses, wine and coffee. In medium-grade-resort and big-town restaurants you pay roughly 120-200$. In really superior establishments allow up to about 400$; and in those with *fado* singers (see p. 71) allow up to at least 350$ a head, with extra for drinks. Many 3-star *pensões* charge only 60-80$ for 4 good courses and coffee.

If you want a quick bite go, if possible, to a snackbar (called 'snackbar' or '*buffete*'). These places serve sandwiches for 25-35$.

In discothèques or *boîtes* (see p. 74) allow up to 100$ for entry and first drink, and about 150$ for dinner (without drink)—if it is served. Nightclubs charge a little more for dinner and floor show than the relatively expensive ordinary restaurants.

Portuguese wines cost about 40-80$ a bottle in restaurants or 15$ to 25$00 for a half-litre carafe. For port and madeira you pay 18-30$ a glass. Imported wines and spirits are also available but are expensive.

A 10% service charge is added to all restaurant bills. It is usual to give a small additional tip of around 5%.

Bars
These are rather more frequent than restaurants. Few serve cooked food, though many, specially in country areas will produce sandwiches if asked. Ordinary bars' prices are about 7.50-10$ for a beer, 7-10$ for a glass of wine, 12-25$ for a brandy, 3$50-6$ for coffee, and 7-9$ for soft drinks. Smart hotel bars naturally charge more than this, as do bars in city centres and popular tourist regions.

Shopping

Most shops are open daily except Sundays from 09.00 to 13.00, and from 15.00 to 17.00. Local times vary however, with shops in smaller towns and tourist centres opening earlier and closing later. All shops close on national holidays, and on some local holidays as well.

You will find lots of very attractive shops in the main towns and tourist resorts, and some excellent boutiques in resorts and de luxe town hotels. Portugal excels in a large variety of craft products— lovely fabrics of every sort, including heavy-weave rugs, blankets, and bedspreads; attractive clothes, especially for children; embroidery of various types, used also on handerkerchiefs, night-dresses, and underwear; marquetry; lace; leather work of every sort, including even handmade shoes, ready in 3 or 4 days (Lisbon and some other big towns); ceramics and ornamental tiles; copper-ware and every sort of metalwork; silver filigree jewellery; and baskets and wickerwork. An unusual item is corkware, which ranges from cork-soled sandals to cork containers for keeping ice cool or food warm.

You can also of course buy local wines and spirits and port and madeira. Wine costs mostly 26-60$ a bottle, ordinary port and madeira 56-120$ (more for special brands). If you bring in additional bottles of still table wine to your customs allowance and declare them (this is important: do not try to avoid paying duty) the wine is still cheaper than if you buy it in Britain. What you pay on spirits and fortified wines makes it not worth the trouble of bringing back more than your duty-free allowance.

Foodstuffs particularly worth buying include Elvas sugar-plums, a preserved fruit very popular in Portugal, and many other locally-produced sweetmeats; olive oil; and honey. If you are camping or caravanning or fending for yourself in a rented villa or flat, you will find shopping for food much more fun than in most parts of Britain. To begin with, it is a social occasion, with friendly greetings and chitchat all round as soon as you show up on the second day. The fact that you speak no Portuguese and the shop or stall people no English doesn't inhibit conversation. And if you are near a fishing port—as you probably will be—you can get an enormous amount of pleasure out of going down to the quayside very early in the morning to buy the fish and shellfish that you most fancy direct from the men who brought it in.

Prices
Portugal, like other countries, has been seriously affected by inflation. This, combined with a decrease in the pound's value, has prevented Portugal being the cheap country it once was for British visitors. The price of food in ordinary supermarkets, for instance, are mostly within a penny or two of what you might expect to pay in Britain. The chief exceptions are local wines, fruit and vegetables, and fresh fish, all of which are still cheap—and good. Cosmetics and toilet goods, most of which are imported, are likely to be expensive and scarce. Sudden shortages, even in basic foodstuffs such as butter, can also occur, because, chiefly, of the uncertain political and economic climate, though things are becoming increasingly more moderate in these areas. As in most

Dresses

British	10	12	14	16	18	20
Continental	40	42	44	46	48	50

Shirts

British	13	13½	14	14½	15	15½	16	16½	17
Continental	33	34	36	37	38	39	41	42	43

Adult shoes

British	3	4	5	6	7	8	9	10
Continental	36	37	38	39	41	42	43	44

Glove and sock sizes are the same as in UK. The same applies to non-stretch tights.

Weights and Measures
Weight The standard weight is the kilogram, which is approximately 2·2 lb.

Kilos	¼	½	1	2	3	5	10	30	50	100	500
Pounds	0·6	1·1	2·2	4·4	6·6	11	22	66	110	220	1100

Liquid The standard liquid measure is the litre, which equals approximately 1¾ pints. There are about 4½ litres to the gallon.

Litres	1	2	3	4	5	10	15	20	30	40	50
Gallons	·2	·4	·7	·9	1·1	2·2	3·3	4·4	6·6	8·8	11

Linear The standard measurement of length is the metre, which is 3 feet 3⅓ inches. There are 100 centimetres to the metre, and 1,000 metres to the kilometre, which is roughly equivalent to ⅝ of a mile.

Centimetres	1	2	3	4	5	10	25	50	100	
Inches	·4	·8	1·2	1·6	2	3·9	9·8	19·7	39·4	
Metres	1	2	3	4	5	10	25	50	100	
Feet	3·3	6·6	9·8	13·1	16·4	32·8	82	164	328·1	
Kms	1	5	10	20	50	100	200	300	400	500
Miles	·6	3·1	6·2	12·4	31·1	62·1	124·3	186·4	248·5	310·7

countries, you can manage quite reasonably when camping or caravanning if you shop around and buy the sort of things the locals eat, rather than what you are accustomed to at home.

Motoring costs—petrol 17$50 for super, 16$50 for ordinary; 25 April Bridge tolls 10-25$; other motorway tolls 5$-7$50; Lisbon ferries 10-20$; Ayamonte ferry—car and driver 50-80$, passengers 8$; overnight lockup garage 20$; car hire from £45 per week for a mini with unlimited mileage, if booked in advance through a British firm (see p. 25).

Clothing sizes

The tables below should be treated with a lot of caution as neither British nor Continental size labelling is sufficiently standardised to guarantee anything but very rough equivalents. In most cases Portuguese shop assistants will be only too pleased to do everything necessary to ensure that your purchases fit properly. Do not hesitate to ask their help.

Tipping

Portuguese wages and salaries are low: hotel staff, for instance, rely on the 10% service charges with a guaranteed minimum in slack seasons. Mainly for that reason it is customary to give extra unless the service has been poor—from 50$ per week to hotel chambermaids and porters (*conierges*) in 1st-class hotels; 10$ to the baggage porter; and an additional 5-10% for meals, drinks, and so on. Where a service charge is not added, give at least 10%. Taxi drivers get 15% of the fare; hairdressers 10% (minimum 8$); cloakroom attendants 3$50; cinema and theatre ushers 2$ per person (minimum 4$); railway and airport porters 5$ per bag.

Emergency and General Information

If you have booked an inclusive holiday, your travel firm's rep will normally give any help you need. In other cases first consult your

hotel. If you have to send a cable asking for money or other help
do not forget to include your full address. If you have to pay out
money which you think you can recover from your insurance
company, make certain that you get clearly-marked receipts for
everything you spend. Spot cash can be a problem if difficulties
arise: do not overlook the uses of credit cards (Diners, Access,
Barclaycard, and so on), which can often be used to pay for
accommodation, meals, air tickets, and other relatively expensive
items; and of bank cards which enable you to draw up to £30 in
cash a day from local banks.

British Consuls and Vice-Consuls are not allowed to give you any
assistance beyond returning you to Britain by the cheapest method
if you cannot pay for your own tickets, and getting you a
temporary travel document if you have lost your passport. They
will, however, give you advice and information in the event of
serious difficulty, such as arrest by the police.

Postal services

	Portugal	UK & Europe	N. America
Postcards	2$00	5$00	5$80
Letters (up to 5 g about $\frac{1}{6}$ oz)	3$00	7$00	7$80

All mail goes by air if that is quicker.

Letter boxes are painted red as in Britain. You buy stamps (*selos*)
from a post office, from a hotel porter, or reception clerk, or from
any shop authorised to sell tobacco. Post restante letters should
be addressed to you at: *Posta-Restante,* followed by the name of
the town and of the province. You must of course take your
passport when collecting post restante letters.

Telephone dialing is automatic to most places inside Portugal.
Local calls from very British-looking call boxes cost 1$50 for 2
minutes, but it is usually easier (except perhaps in Lisbon) to go
into any bar and pay 2$. You are not expected to buy drinks
when making phone calls. Long-distance calls cost up to about
20$ for 3 minutes. Calls to London—80$ for 3 minutes.

WCs Go into any bar or snackbar and ask for the *toilette*
(pronounced roughly as in French). No need to buy anything. If
there is an attendant, give her about 2$. Except in the remotest
areas lavatories, like everything else in Portugal, are very clean.
Apart from *toilette* the signs may say: WC, *lavabo,* or *retrete.*
Ladies is *Senhoras,* Gentlemen is *Homens.*

Churches

Anglican churches: St George's, Rua de São Jorge Estrela 4,
Lisbon; St James's, Largo de Maternidade Juliu Dinis, Porto;
St Paul's, Avenida dos Bombeiros Voluntarios 1, Estoril; St

Sebastian's Chapel, Cascais; Parish Church, Carcavelos; St
Vincent's, Quinta do Rei, Praia da Rocha.
Church of Scotland: St Andrew's, Rua da Arriaga 11, Lisbon.
Catholic services in English: Corpo Santo, Travessa do Corpo
Santo, Lisbon; many other Catholic churches hold occasional
services in English for visitors. Enquire at local Turismo office.
Other denominations: Several have regular services in Lisbon and
occasional ones elsewhere. Enquire at Lisbon and local Turismo
offices.

Warning

Don't pick the oranges! Even if you are excited as most Britons
are at seeing oranges actually growing on trees, do not pick those
you see in public places such as streets and squares. The fruit here
is reserved for distribution to needy families and there is a 500$
fine, payable on the nail, for unauthorised scrumping of local
authorities' fruit.

Sources of Information

In Britain

Information and visas:

Portuguese National Tourist Office, 1-5 New Bond Street, London
 W1

Portuguese Consulate-General, 47 Wilton Crescent, London SW1
 (consulates also in Cardiff, Liverpool, and Southampton)

In Portugal

British Embassy & Consulate-General, 35-39 Rua San Domingos
a Lapa, Lisbon: tel. 661.191

British Consulate, Avenida da Boavista 307: tel. 684.789
 (consular representatives also at Figueira da Foz, Vila Real
 de Santo António, and Portimão)

British Airways, Avenida da Liberdade 23-27, Lisbon

TAP, Praça Marques de Pombal 3, Lisbon

British Caledonian, Avenida da Liberdade 227, Lisbon

British Airways & TAP, Rua Dom Francisco Gomes 8, Faro *and*
 Praca Dona Felipe de Lencastre 1-3, Porto

Most towns have tourist information offices marked Turismo.

National Holidays

These are partly Catholic religious feasts and partly celebrations of
national events.

January 1	New Year's Day
April 25	Portuguese National Day
May 1	Labour Day
(varies)	Corpus Christi
June 10	National Day
August 15	Assumption

October 5	Anniversary of the Declaration of the Republic
November 1	All Saints' Day
December 1	Independence Day
December 8	Feast of the Immaculate Conception
December 25	Christmas Day

Though not officially holidays, Shrove Tuesday (the Tuesday before the start of Lent), Maundy Thursday (Thursday before Good Friday) and Good Friday are treated as such by lots of people. Many shops close on these days. Note that Easter Monday and Boxing Day are not official holidays. Shops may also close on days when local festivals are being held. A short list is given below.

Aveiro	Boat festival, with processions and competitions—lasts 1 month starting March 25.
Braga	Romaria and processions—last Sunday in August.
Coimbra	Queima das Fitas (colourful end of university year festival)—mid-May.
Évora	Goblets Fair (religious processions and sale of local pottery)—February 2nd-3rd.
Fátima	Pilgrimage on the 12th-13th of every month from May to October; biggest gatherings in May and October.
Figueira da Foz	Feast of St John—June 23rd-24th.
Guimarães	Gualterianas (Feast of St Walter: processions, bullfights, fireworks)—1st Sunday in August.
Lisbon	Festivals include mass marriages at the Cathedral on June 13th.
Loulé	Almond Gatherers' Fair (4 days) coincides with Carnival, starting on the Saturday before Shrove Tuesday.
Miranda do Douro	Romaria to Our Lady of Nazo (11 km north: renowned Pauliteiros stick dance, etc)—Sept. 7th-8th.
Nazaré	Festival of Our Lady of Nazareth (folk music, folk-dancing, bullfights)—mid-Sept.
Oporto	Feasts of St John and St Peter (torchlight performances, fireworks)—June 24th and 29th.
Póvoa de Varzim	Blessing of the fishing boats (processions, fireworks)—August 15th.
Santarém	Feira of Our Lady of Sorrow—2nd Sunday in October (lasts 2 weeks).

Sesimbra	Festival of Our Lady of the Wounds (fishermen's processions, fireworks)—May 5th.
Setúbal	St James's Fair (folk music, folkdancing, bullfights, fireworks)—July 25th-August 8th.
Viana do Castelo	Romaria of Our Lady of the Agony—Friday nearest August 20th (lasts 3 days).

Charges

Sport

Golf—green fees vary from 200$ to 300$.

Tennis—courts cost 20-50$ per hour.

Sea-fishing—no licence needed: boats cost 1,500-4,500$ per day for 4 people, equipment and meals included.

Riding—90-100$ per hour.

Underwater fishing—no licence needed.

Scuba diving—no licence needed.

Freshwater fishing—licences cost 5$, but are not needed by foreign visitors.

Hunting licences—deposit of 1000$ required at frontier.

Museum and art gallery opening times and charges

Most museums and art galleries open from 10.00 (occasionally 9.00 or 11.00) to 17.00, sometimes with a break at lunchtime (maximum 12.00-14.00 but usually less). They close mostly only on Monday (occasionally Tuesday) and on public holidays. Admission charge is usually about 5$. Saturday and Sunday are sometimes free.

Motoring and Camping

Driving in Portugal is pleasant. Apart from short stretches of motorway and some new highways, roads are neither wide nor fast, and a few stretches are bumpy and cobbled. But except in big-city rush hours traffic is decidedly light—a very welcome change. However, it brings a minor problem of its own: like all drivers on empty roads (including you and me) the Portuguese may become careless. But they are not aggressive and their driving is a good deal less frightening than in many countries.

A major point to keep in mind is that, apart from a few relatively busy roads near Lisbon and the main road north to Oporto, nearly all Portugal's roads are mountain roads. After coming over a high range you often think you are coming to level ground. But you are not: you simply twist and turn at a lower level.

Documents. To take your car into Portugal for up to 1 year you need the registration book (log book) and your driving licence—not a provisional one, of course. If the car is not registered in your name you must have a letter of authority from the registered owner certified by the AA or RAC. If you cannot take the log book—if the car is hired, for instance—a complicated Department of the Environment certification is needed which the RAC and AA will see to for members. Third-party insurance is not compulsory, but it is obviously advisable to have a 'green card'—a document certifying that your insurance cover has been extended to Portugal and other countries you may be driving through. You obtain this for a usually small sum (charges vary) from your own insurance company. Apply in good time.

To drive through Spain you will need also an international driving permit (£1.50 from the AA or RAC: take or send a passport photograph and your national licence) and a 'bail bond' from your insurers. The latter saves you being jailed and your car impounded pending the settlement of any court action or legal claim against you, following an accident in Spain. The bail bond is issued automatically and without charge along with the green card, if you tell your insurance company you are visiting Spain.

Additional Insurance The green card extends your UK insurance to other countries. It does not cover extra costs that may occur after accidents or breakdowns, such as flying out spare parts, paying for additional hotels, or for air tickets home, and so on. Such risks are covered by policies issued by Lloyd's, the AA, RAC, Europ Assistance, Thomas Cook Ltd, and, for caravan owners, the Caravan Club. It is well worth writing round for sample policies and comparing them. Addresses on p. 4.

Rules of the Road

In Portugal you drive on the right and overtake on the left (except trams). Apart from the motorway near Lisbon and on clearly marked priority roads you give way to all traffic coming from your right (unless from a private drive). Remember that you will often have priority over vehicles on your left.

You are not obliged to modify your headlights. But it is a nuisance for everyone, including yourself, if they dip left instead of right. The easiest way of altering this is to buy a set of yellow lenses from your garage, a car accessory shop, or the AA or RAC. . . . If you are coming through Spain carry a full set of spare lamps to save a possible on-the-spot fine for not having all your compulsory lamps in working order.

Warning triangles are compulsory in Portugal. They must be placed 30 m (35 yds) behind the car and be visible from 100 m— unless the stopped car is itself visible from 100 m. Hooting is forbidden in built-up areas, and the ban is respected. It is not compulsory to hoot before overtaking when outside towns (as it is in some countries), but it is not a bad idea.

As in most Continental countries you are legally obliged to carry your car documents, driving licence, and personal identity documents with you at all times. Police operate quite frequent spot checks and you must, of course, produce insurance certificate, driving licence, and passport if involved in an accident.

Remember that on-the-spot fines can be imposed by the police for most straightforward traffic offences, such as wrong parking, exceeding the speed limit, etc. Penalties for driving under the influence of alcohol are severe.

Speed limits in built-up areas are 60 kmph (37 mph) for cars without trailers and 50 kmph (31 mph) with trailers. Outside towns 90 kmph (55 mph) on main roads, 70 kmph (43 mph) with trailers, and 120 kmph (75 mph) on motorways, are the respective speed limits.

Parking restrictions are precise. You must not park on a bridge, within 5 m of a bend or tram stop, within 10 m of a bus stop, in front of a driveway or entrance to a public park, school, church, or theatre, on the brow of a hill, or within 30 m of a road junction or crossroads. Nor, of course, where there are 'No Parking' signs. Parking discs, obtainable free from police stations and some tourist information offices, must be used in Lisbon and other towns with a 'blue zone' (*zona azul*).

Road standards are sound, though not outstanding. Sections paved with basalt setts should be treated with very great caution after light rain, when they become terrifyingly slippery. When completely dry they are safe, but noisy and therefore tiring.

Tolls are payable on short lengths of motorway near Lisbon, on the 25 April Bridge over the Tagus in Lisbon, and of course on the Tagus ferries (see p. 17).

Road signs in general follow the Continental pattern. One speciality however is the use of speed limit signs by themselves to warn you of obstructions ahead, such as narrow bridges or ramps. If you meet a 30 km sign just before a blind corner, take it seriously. Roads are numbered and the numbers prefixed with N (for *nacional*). You are not likely to drive on non-national roads unless visiting friends in very out-of-the-way country homes.

Directional signposting is fairly good on major roads. The next main town and the road number are normally clearly posted at exits from towns. Rather oddly, however, the main destination often is not repeated at turnings off the main road. On side roads, signposting often peters out after you have left the major route. Signs vanish in towns. The Michelin 37 (Portugal) is essential for serious motoring.

Accidents In general take action as in Britain. Have the police called if anyone is injured. Above all, try to get names and addresses of witnesses. After an accident provide your name and address by showing your British driving licence (also your passport) and allow any interested person to copy your insurance company's name and address from your insurance certificate. The UK document usually shows it more clearly than the green card.

Petrol stations and garages are plentiful enough on main roads. Manufacturers' accredited agents can be found in Lisbon, Oporto, and some other towns. Repairs are usually carefully done. You may however consider it worth while to hire a spare parts pack through your garage or the AA or RAC, who will also advise you on what to take.

Getting There

Calais, Boulogne, Le Touquet, Dieppe, Le Havre, and Cherbourg are the best ports to make for. They are served by Sealink, Townsend-Thoresen, Seaspeed, Hoverlloyd, and Normandy Ferries. Harwich may also be a suitable port if you are starting from East Anglia, the Midlands, or further north.

The key point to head for in France is Bordeaux. From Ostend, Calais, Boulogne, or Le Touquet join the northern motorway to Paris. Circle the city anti-clockwise by the dual-carriageway boulevard périphérique and leave by the A13/A12/N10 for

Chartres, Bordeaux, and Biarritz to the Spanish frontier at
Hendaye. From Dieppe and Le Havre join either the A13 at
Rouen or the N10 at Chartres or Tours. From Cherbourg head for
Angers and the N10 at Poitiers. A good and up-to-date map of
France is essential because of current new road construction. The
Michelin 989 is recommended.

An easy route inside Spain is via Burgos (NI), Valladolid,
Salamanca, and Fuentes de Oñoro (N620). From Salamanca you
can also continue south to Cáceres (N630), and turn west on the
N521 for Lisbon (N16 inside Portugal); or to Mérida (still N630)
where you turn west on the NV (N4 inside Portugal) to Lisbon.
Spanish-Portuguese frontier posts are all open 8.00-21.00, extended
at main points in summer to 7.00-midnight or 7.00-1.00. Yet
another possibility is to drive via Madrid (NI), Córdoba and Seville
(NIV), and Ayamonte (N431), where you cross the River
Guadiana by ferry direct to the Algarve coast. For ferry costs
see p. 17.

Short Cuts You can cut down driving by taking the Swedish Lloyd
ferry service to Bilbao (37 hours), or Aznar's to Santander (33 hours)
from Southampton. Bilbao is about 510 miles from Lisbon. For
prices see p. 8. From Bilbao you can travel south to Burgos and
then as above. Or you can take the slow, strenuous, but very
attractive coast roads (N634, etc) past Santander and Oviedo to
Corunna (La Coruña in Spanish), where you turn south through
Santiago de Compostela and Vigo (N550) and enter Portugal at
Valença do Minho. Both routes involve a 400-mile drive to the
Portuguese border. From Santander you can take either of the
routes mentioned above, or cross the fine Pajares pass south of
Oviedo and then through Leon and Zamora. You can of course
take one ferry out and a different one home.

Car-sleeper trains from Boulogne, Dieppe, Rouen, and Paris to
Biarritz will also shorten your journey. Other useful car-sleepers
link Paris or Irun and Madrid. Most operate only on certain days
from April to October. Information can be obtained from French
Railways, Sealink, certain main BR stations, travel agents, and,
for the Paris-Madrid service, the Spanish National Tourist Office
in London.

Car Hire in Portugal

Self-drive cars can be hired in Portugal by the hour, day, week,
or month in most places where there is a fair number of tourists
(specimen price p. 17). However it is well worth making arrangements in advance if possible. This is best done through the
organisation—airline, travel agent, and so on—you travel by, or

through an international car-hire concern such as Hertz. In addition, some firms offer package holidays that include air fares and car hire, with hotel reservations if required. See p. 9.

Picturesque Roads

Almost everywhere you drive in Portugal you will find yourself giving exclamations of delight every few minutes—the only exceptions to the beautiful scenery being some of the areas round Lisbon, Oporto, much of the Estremadura province, and parts of the Algarve—until you drive through the towns and villages. The Michelin map of Portugal (No. 37) prints a green border to all roads considered picturesque—and there is more green border on the Michelin 37 than on any other map in the series. Even where green is scarce, notably in the vast Alentejo province, you will find the scenery very attractive and the villages extraordinarily colourful. Three really outstanding drives are outlined in our What To See section under Douro Valley, Serra da Estrela, and Sintra.

Road Distance Chart: distances in km by main through roads

Town	From		
	Lisbon	Oporto	Faro
Aveiro	275	78	581
Beja	189	388	154
Braga	365	50	671
Bragança	544	251	850
Castelo Branco	268	271	329
Coimbra	199	116	502
Elvas	222	506	394
Estoril	27	350	330
Évora	142	457	205
Faro	304	619	—
Guarda	365	223	488
Lisbon	—	315	304
Nazaré	118	230	422
Oporto	315	—	619
Portalegre	233	360	306
Santarém	77	225	285
Sintra	28	320	334
Viana do Castelo	385	70	789
Viseu	277	138	469

Tyre Pressure Equivalents

lb per in²	16	18	20	21	22	23	24	25	26	27
kg per cm²	1·13	1·27	1·41	1·48	1·55	1·62	1·69	1·76	1·83	1·90
lb per in²	28	30								
kg per cm²	1·97	2·11								

As garages' tyre pressure gauges cannot measure ·01 kg per cm²
use round figures—'one-five' or 'one-five hundred' (to use the
common expressions) for 21 lb per in², for instance, and 'two' for
a 28 lb pressure.

For litre-gallon and gallon-litre equivalents see p. 16.

Camping and Caravanning

Portugal's climate provides a long season during which camping
and caravanning is thoroughly enjoyable. If you wish you can
camp or park your van on any land, with the owner's permission,
that is not inside a built-up area, in a protected water-supply zone,
on a beach or other public open space, or within 1 km (just over
½ mile) from an organised campsite. Well equipped sites, however,
are available in many spots of general tourist interest. They are
more frequent in the north. But there are enough everywhere to
enable car-campers and caravanners to see and enjoy every part
of the country. A list giving details of available facilities can be
obtained free from the Portuguese National Tourist Office. All
sites accept trailer and motor caravans. Prices are extremely
reasonable.

Camping carnets and membership of camping or caravanning
clubs are not essential. They are however advisable as they provide
third-party insurance for damage you may do to other people's
property, and serve also as introductions to sites owned and run
by local clubs and other private bodies, such as the Portuguese
Camping and Caravanning Federation (Federacão Portuguesa de
Campismo e Caravanismo). An organisation called Orbitur runs
about 15 of the better sites. Many others belong to local
authorities or local tourist associations. Campsites are called
parques de campismo in Portuguese.

Trailer-caravanners intending to tour Portugal would be well
advised to study the map carefully before leaving so as to avoid
too much towing on narrow, uneven, winding, and often steep
mountain roads. If you are keeping to coastal regions, few
problems arise. But if you want to explore the interior, choose a

limited number of bases reachable by the wider and less winding roads and make day excursions from them. The Michelin 37 shows road widths and indicates pretty clearly which roads are packed tight with bends.

Azulejos decoration at the University Chapel of Coimbra (p. 33)

What to See

History

Portugal's early history corresponds to that of all the western Mediterranean region. First came the establishment of Phoenician and Greek coastal trading posts (from the 9th and 6th centuries BC respectively), then involvement in Rome's Phoenician (or 'Punic') wars against Carthage in the 3rd and 2nd centuries, and finally conquest by Rome and incorporation into the prosperous Roman Empire. The country's modern history begins with Rome's collapse and the Visigoth invasion of the 5th century AD.

Portugal's present 9 million inhabitants are descended very largely from the Lusitanian tribes who were there when the Phoenicians first arrived, from the Romans who settled there for nearly 700 years, and from invading Visigoth tribes. The close-packed mountain ranges which make up most of Portugal—not high, but a barrier to easy communications—and the sea, have kept Portugal largely isolated till modern times, even from her Spanish neighbours. The country has developed on distinctive lines.

In AD 711 a 'Moorish' army made up of Arabs and Islamised Berbers invaded Spain and Portugal from North Africa, and overran almost the whole Iberian Peninsula. It was from the Asturias, a part of north-west Spain not effectively conquered by the Moors, that the reconquest of Portugal began. It started early —much earlier than in Spain. By the 9th century the county of 'Portucale' (from the Latin *Portus Cale,* see p. 56) was in Christian hands, and the country still called 'Portugal' had begun its existence. By 1147 its boundaries had been extended south to Lisbon. In 1249 the extreme southern province of the Algarve (Arabic *al-Gharb* means 'the west') was recaptured and the last Moors expelled.

The foundation of a university in Lisbon in 1290 (moved to Coimbra in 1308), with teachers drawn from Bologna, Oxford, Salamanca, Paris, and elsewhere, made Portugal one of Europe's most famous centres of learning.

A little over a century later, the capture of Ceuta, some 40 miles east of Tangier on Morocco's Mediterranean coast, began a century of expansion and exploration in which Portugal's seamen led the world and discovered much that no Europeans had previously seen. The purpose of Ceuta's capture was to make Moorish raids on Portuguese shipping more difficult. The real mainspring of Portuguese exploration, however, was the scientific advances in shipbuilding, map-making, and navigation that resulted from the school of navigation established by Prince Henry the Navigator on the windswept, flat clifftop looking across to

Cape St Vincent, near Sagres. It is an inspiring spot, which you can still visit.

Improved navigational instruments were developed here, making it possible to fix positions exactly by the stars for the first time. Far better charts than other nations possessed were drawn. A new type of sea-going vessel, the caravel, was produced. Its shallow draught and stern rudder ensured manageability; its wide, enclosed hull provided more shelter than crews had been accustomed to; and its several masts, instead of just one, ensured a considerable spread of sail and greater speed as well as ability to tack against the wind.

Madeira was discovered in 1420, and the Azores in 1427. In 1434 a Portuguese ship sailed further down Africa's west coast than any modern European had previously been. The mouth of the River Congo was reached in 1482, and Brazil in 1500. Meanwhile Columbus, refused help in Portugal, had discovered the New World for the rulers of Spanish Castile in 1492.

Prince Henry had died in 1460 but his work went on. Bartolomeu Dias, reached Tempest Cape in 1488, renamed Cape of Good Hope by the Portuguese King. Ten years later Vasco da Gama had reached Mozambique and India. By 1540 commercial relations were being established with China, Siam, and Indonesia. The Portuguese route to the orient was protected by a number of fortified posts. Portugal had not only achieved a monopoly of the Far Eastern trade, previously run by Turks and Arabs, but she had also diverted much of the trade that previously passed through Mediterranean ports such as Venice and Genoa, or through the Baltic ports, to her own harbours, mainly Lisbon. Spain, with vast colonial possessions in the New World, was her great rival.

For a tiny country this was a fantastic achievement. But it turned out an exhausting one. Wealth poured into the country, but people and skills flowed out. The population decreased from 2 million to 1 million; the land stopped being properly cultivated; craftsmen went elsewhere; and much newly-won wealth was dissipated in paying for imports. An attempt to lead a sort of Crusade against Moslem North Africa—part of its object was to find the fabled Christian kingdom, beyond the Moslem lands, ruled by the legendary Prester John, and to exploit its presumed wealth—ended Portugal's power and also its independence.

Philip II of Spain invaded and conquered the country in 1580 and had himself crowned Philip I of Portugal. But the Portuguese were never content to be ruled by Spain. In 1640 the Duke of Braganza rebelled, and assumed the title of King John IV of Portugal. The marriage of his daughter Catherine to Charles II of England in 1662 was an indication of Portuguese-British understanding: it,

incidentally, gave Tangier and Bombay, part of her dowry, to
Britain. In 1668 Spain recognised Portugal's independence. The
dynasty established by John of Braganza continued to rule
Portugal till 1910. John himself was descended from the earlier
line of Portuguese kings begun in 1386 by João I and his Queen,
Philippa, daughter of England's John of Gaunt.

In 1703 England and Portugal signed a commercial treaty, the
Methuen Treaty, by which British woollens were exchanged for
Portuguese port wine. In 1755 a terrible earthquake devastated
Lisbon (see p. 36) causing a huge amount of damage elsewhere.

By the turn of the century Portugal and Britain were jointly facing
revolutionary France. In 1808 British troops under Wellington
landed in Portugal to help expel the French invaders. Six years
later, after a series of brilliant but very hard campaigns, Portugal
was again free. But war's impoverishment brought discontent,
intrigue, and civil war, which lasted till 1834. Meanwhile Brazil,
Portugal's richest possession, had become independent in 1828.

Discontent continued in various forms through the 19th century
and culminated with the assassination of both the king and the heir
to the throne in 1908. The Republic declared in 1910 was however
unable to achieve stability, though it sent a force to help the Allies
against Germany in 1916.

A critical economic situation in the late 1920s and early 1930s led
to a seizure of power in 1932 by Dr Oliveira Salazar, who had
been Minister of Finance since 1928. As President from 1932 to
his retirement in 1968, Dr Salazar ruled Portugal with a very firm
hand. The dictatorial form of government he established formally
in 1933 survived until 25 April 1974 when it collapsed under a
sudden upsurge of popular feeling, led by the army. The country
held its first free parliamentary election for nearly half a century
in 1975.

Portugal today, despite modern developments, is still a mainly
agricultural country. Some 30% of the working population is
engaged in farming. Cereals, vines, olives, fruit and vegetables,
cattle and other stock, and timber—especially cork, for Portugal
can claim one-third of all the world's cork oaks—are the main
products. But the land is not fertile. The sea still supplements the
nation's income and its food resources. Over 30,000 men are
engaged in fishing and ten times as much fish as meat is eaten in
Lisbon. Portugal's merchant navy transports much of her overseas
trade, including that with overseas territories such as the Azores
and Mozambique, which are still Portuguese.

Mining occupies an important place in the industrial field. It
produces iron ore, uranium, tungsten, tin, and other metals,

together with marble, granite, and slate. Many mineral resources, however, are still not being exploited. Manufacturing industries include oil refining, ironworks, fertiliser factories, car assembly plants, wiremills, cotton and wool weaving mills, cork-making plants, and canneries for fish and other products. Industrial development is linked to the increased supply of hydro-electric power. Over 30 dams have been built in 30 years and capacity is expected to double within the next 10. A quarter of the country's total population already lives in the industrialised areas around Lisbon and Oporto. But despite growing industrialisation and an inevitable drift to the towns, as well as the increased importance of tourism, Portugal remains a delightfully 'unspoilt' country.

Architecture

Specifically Portuguese styles began to emerge even before the country became independent. Romanesque churches were built in granite in northern regions during the 11th and 12th centuries. Cathedrals of this style and date were constructed to be as much fortresses as places of worship: the one at Coimbra is a notable example. Portuguese Gothic flourished during the 13th and 14th centuries, especially in the area near Lisbon: the churches and monasteries to be seen at Santarém, Alcobaça, and Batalha are outstanding examples. As Gothic began to merge into Renaissance, Portugal developed the most distinctive of all its architectural styles, called Manueline because it flourished in the reign of Manuel I (1490-1520). It was magnificently imaginative and decorative, using everything from flowers, leaves, corncobs, and even artichokes to anchors, globes, and ropes as models for its sculpture. The most famous example is the window designed by Diogo de Arruda in the Convent of Christ at Tomar. In the 16th century, too, Spanish Plateresque style—exceptionally rich reliefs carved in the manner of silversmiths' work (Spanish *platero* means silversmith)—appeared in Portugal. In the same way, in earlier years, there had been examples of what are called by the Spanish names Mudejar and Mozarabic styles. The first is applied to Christian buildings in which Moorish influence can be traced, and the second to the work of Christian craftsmen done for Moorish masters or under Moorish inspiration. During the Manueline period a new development along these lines was the 'Luso-Moorish' style evolved by Francisco de Arruda, brother of the Tomar window designer.

Though Portugal's prosperity and independence disappeared before the end of the 16th century, architecture continued to flourish through the Classical and Baroque periods of the 17th and 18th centuries. Fine examples of baroque can be seen in Lisbon,

Oporto, Braga, Mafra, and elsewhere.

Apart from the many examples of religious architecture,
Portugal's castles deserve special study. The earliest, such as the
one which crowns the lovely northern walled town of Bragança
and those at Guimarães, and Leiria, were built to establish control
over territory reconquered from the Moors. Those built or rebuilt
from the 13th to 17th century guarded main roads: the ones at
Estremoz, Evoramonte, and elsewhere are good examples. Finally
a number were built or rebuilt at places such as Elvas, in the 17th
century, to defend the frontier with Spain.

Windmills and watermills survive in many places, and the traditional house-building styles of every region that are one of
Portugal's most fascinating and attractive features, varying from
the low, whitewashed, almost windowless cottages of the southern
Alentejo province, with their huge chimneys, to the small granite-
built Minho homes where broad staircases lead up to first-floor
verandas large enough to be used as open-air sitting rooms.
Elegant small Moorish-style chimneys are a distinctive feature of
the Algarve's small white houses.

Rather surprisingly, beautifully designed old pillories are frequent.
These were erected in every place which had the right to hold
courts and administer justice. They consist of a single column, to
which the cage containing a criminal was attached in bygone days,
often topped by a decoration based on the cage theme.

Around the middle of the 14th century Portugal began to manufacture *azulejos*—decorative tiles, at first in geometric patterns,
based on a blue (*azul*) background. Moorish tiles had been
'discovered' when Ceuta was captured in 1415, and imported from
Morocco, or the Moorish province of Andalusia in southern
Spain, for 150 years. But after about 1580 Portugal manufactured
her own and a positive craze for them lasted until the end of the
18th century: you see the results all over the country. Geometric
patterns were soon abandoned in favour of elaborate and beautiful
pictures covering large areas of wall. At the beginning of the craze
many tiles were imported from Delft and other Dutch sources.

The Country

If holidays for you mean lovely sandy beaches, good accommodation and plentiful evening entertainment, together with
things like riding, snorkelling, scuba diving, tennis, sea-fishing,
underwater fishing, and first-rate golf, Portugal can meet all your
needs. The two main sections of coast catering primarily for
foreign visitors are the long-established Costa do Sol (Sun Coast),
west of Lisbon, with Estoril and Cascais its main resorts, and the

fast-developing Algarve coast, where hotels were not built until the early 1960s. Each of these regions has a distinctive character. Even together, however, they contain only a fraction of Portugal's total 850 km (530 miles) of sand. Inclusive-tour firms now include a good selection of lesser-known but very attractive resorts.

Beaches and coast resorts, however, are only the start. Portugal possesses an extraordinary and little-appreciated abundance of old towns—places like Bragança, Evora, Estremoz, Lagos and many others—and numerous magnificent medieval monasteries and palaces. Its scenery, too, is outstanding. Most people do not realise that Portugal is extremely mountainous. Though peaks are not specially high, the mountain ranges are all but continuous. It makes car touring, in particular, a constant delight.

Vegetation deserves a special note. Portugal is unique in present-ing, in its tiny space, trees and shrubs and cultivated crops belong-ing to every sort of climate from North European to tropical (see Sintra and Bussaco). The innumerable cultivated gardens are naturally magnificent.

The country's different regions vary strikingly, even though tiny Portugal would fit comfortably into a rectangle of only 600 km (375 miles) by 240 km (150 miles). The variations are roughly embodied in the ancient provinces' boundaries.

In the north the Minho province (modern administrative districts of Viana do Castelo and Braga) is filled with tight-packed granite hills, densely wooded, and its little-known beaches are magnificent. Inland Trás-os-Montes, which means 'Beyond the Mountains', (administrative districts of Bragança and Vila Real) consists mainly of a high plateau cut by deep valleys. It is Portugal's remotest area.

Douro, south of the Minho, comprises a small, mostly moun-tainous area round Oporto and is noted, like the Minho, for its vinho verde (see pp. 46 and 47) and its folklore. Inland, Beira Alta (Guarda and Viseu) and Beira Baixa (Castelo Branco), east and south-east of Douro, are the most mountain-filled areas of a mountainous country: it is a sheep and cattle region, with numerous towns and villages built in the shelter of ancient hilltop castles, and with modern dams providing new sources of power and wealth. To all this Beira Litoral (Aveiro and Coimbra) provides a striking contrast. Much is low-lying and the shore consists of miles and miles of lovely white sand.

In the central area, Estremadura (Lisbon, Leiria, and Setúbal) was once Christian Portugal's 'extremity', as its name implies. Except for the Serra de Sintra and the Arrábida range, it is a region of rolling hills where you can see many of the country's most important ancient abbeys, palaces, and towns, including the capital. Its coast, broken by sporadic cliffs, includes Nazaré, Setúbal, and the long-established resorts of Estoril and Cascais. Inland from here the province of Ribatejo (Santarém) lies across the Tagus's lower valley. It is flattish alluvial land where fighting bulls are reared, and all manner of crops grown from vines to rice and vegetables.

The Alentejo is Portugal's largest province, covering a third of the country's total territory and divided into Alto or Upper (Portalegre and Evora) and Baixo or Lower (Beja). The Alentejo is often described as completely flat, which is quite untrue, as every car driver soon discovers. Castles and fortified towns perch on its higher hilltops; the big landowners' large, whitewashed farms, appropriately called *montes* ('hills'), occupy lower crests. Where the rolling open landscapes are not filled with grain crops they are thickly sprinkled with either cork or olive trees.

Separated from the Alentejo by a line of attractive low hills, the tiny, relatively flat Algarve is a world apart, a world of almonds and carobs, oranges, lemons, geraniums, aloes, agaves, sugar, cotton, and rice. Its tiny houses, though also painted white, are wholly different from the Alentejo's. The last bit of Portugal to be reconquered from the Moors, its towns and villages spread up the hillsides almost indistinguishably from the many 'white towns' of northern Morocco, founded, in some cases, by 13th-century Moorish refugees from the Algarve. Moorish influence is obvious too in the province's very distinctive and decorative chimney stacks and in relics such as the vast Moorish castle at Silves. And fringing its coast is another collection of lovely sandy beaches, the basis for large and rapidly growing tourist-residential developments like Vilamoura and Vale de Lobo, as well as some smaller centres.

Despite their differences, all provinces have two things in common —outstandingly friendly people and reasonable prices. And if you wonder why all these delights are only now becoming really popular the answer is simple—Portugal is only just beginning to have enough accommodation to cater for large-scale tourism. Even today it is hardly over-crowded with holiday-makers.

Lisbon

Lisbon is one of Europe's most beautiful cities. It lies on a number of south-facing low hills sloping down to the River Tagus at a point where the estuary is particularly wide and well-sheltered. The city's old medieval centre, Alfama, looks down on the modern centre to its west—the Baixa (Lower Town)—and across the Baixa to the Bairro Alto, with its lively shops and nightclubs. The main modern docks are at Alcántara, still further west, and beyond them at Belém superb 15th to 16th-century buildings mark the site of an older shipping centre. Today, though the city and its one million inhabitants have spread northward far from the river's bank, the Tagus has quaysides stretching all along the city's edge and it is still the artery that carries Lisbon's lifeblood.

Lisbon in fact owes its existence and its importance to its superlative harbour. First occupied by Phoenicians some 3,000 years ago, it was in Roman hands for nearly six centuries and was a Moorish stronghold for four. It became part of Portugal in 1147, and in 1255 replaced Coimbra as the country's capital. In the 15th and early 16th centuries, at the time of the great discoveries, the city grew enormously in wealth and size, and was the starting-place for many notable voyages. Outstanding buildings at Belém recall those days of greatness. Lisbon once possessed many more buildings from the same period, but they were destroyed in the disastrous earthquake of 1755: on November 1st, while virtually the whole town was at High Mass, a violent earth tremor brought churches, houses, and other buildings crashing down. As fire spread through the ruins the survivors rushed to take refuge on the river. As they did so a huge tidal wave came upstream and engulfed the lower town. Some 40,000 of Lisbon's inhabitants were killed on that day.

Yet this same disaster allowed Lisbon to acquire much of its modern charm. For King José I's chief minister, later given the title of Marquis of Pombal, rebuilt the Baixa in a wholly revolutionary style. He conceived and laid out the straight streets inland from the Praça do Comercio and also built the elegant houses you still see today. He gave Lisbon, too, the magnificent Avenida da Liberdade, linking the squares inland from the Baixa to the Praça Marquês de Pombal named in his honour. Other areas, too, were laid out in similar manner, and Lisbon was endowed with an elegance that has been continued into modern times.

The city today has spread a long way north and east from the original central districts, and it is still growing. A whole range of new industries have been developed upstream towards Vila Franca de Xira, and the harbour and shipyards have spread to the Tagus's opposite bank.

The best place to start your sightseeing tour of Lisbon is undoubtedly the waterfront square officially called the Praça do Comercio, known to the Portuguese as Terreiro do Paço (Palace Terrace) from the former royal palace, and to the British and some other nationalities as Black Horse Square, because of the equestrian statue of King José I in its centre. As you stand here facing the Tagus, the bustling Sul e Sueste Station lies to your left front. The palace and the Baixa are behind you, the Cathedral, with Alfama beyond it, to your left, and the Bairro Alto behind and to your right. You can quickly get the feel of Lisbon by walking up one of the streets leading directly inland, such as the Rua Áurea or the Rua Augusta. Both lead into the busy square called the Rossio, with the Rossio Station, just beyond on the left. From the Rossio you pass straight on into the equally lively Praça dos Restauradores, with the Turismo office on your left, and the entrance to a very useful underground car park as well as to the most central of Lisbon's underground stations on the right. Without any break, Restauradores leads into the 1500-metre long and 90-metre wide Avenida da Liberdade (1 mile by almost 100 yards).

Avenida da Liberdade, Lisbon

A through road, flanked by gardens, runs down the middle, while the side roads are used by local traffic, including Lisbon's British-built double-decker buses. Shops, banks, offices, travel agents, and exchange offices fill all this area.

On your way up the Rua Aurea you will have passed a lift (Elevador) connecting with a high bridge leading to the Bairro Alto, and just beyond the Turismo office a funicular carries you up over the railway tunnel. The Bairro Alto itself is a sort of minor Baixa, noted chiefly for its nightspots and restaurants. The Rua Garrett, however, running downhill from the Largo do Chiado and usually called the Chiado, is Lisbon's Bond Street. Here you can see all the city's smartest shops and smartest people.

Medieval Lisbon can be enjoyed by going down the Rua da
Madalena (parallel with the Rua Aurea on the Baixa's eastern
edge) and bearing left up the hill at its end. This takes you past
the Cathedral—built as a fortress at the end of the 12th century
like those in Oporto, Coimbra, and Evora—and on along the Rua
Barão to the Miradouro de Santa Luzia (St Lucia Belvedere).
There is a good view from here of the little medieval streets,
houses and churches of ancient Lisbon. From the belvedere you
can go inland to St George's Castle (Castelo de São Jorge) or
wander on through the narrow streets and stepped alleys of the
colourful old houses of Alfama. This, the city's oldest part, still
retains much of the layout it had during the Moorish occupation,
before the numerous churches—still there—were built. Parts of the
Moorish town wall can still be seen.

In the Largo das Portas do Sol (Sun Gate Square: the Sun Gate
was one of the entrances to the Moorish city) the Fundação
Ricardo Espirito Santa Silva, also called the Museum of
Decorative Art, contains particularly interesting collections of
17th and 18th-century Portuguese and Indo-Portuguese furnishings,
housed in a 17th-century palace.

Belém, west of the city centre, can be reached quickly by the road
running beside the Tagus (take a taxi or a No. 15 tram from
Black Horse Square if you do not have a car). The Belém Tower,
the Jerónimos Monastery, the Museum of Ancient Art (Museu de
Arte Antiga), the Museum of Popular Art (Museu de Arte
Popular), and the modern monument to the Discoveries (Padrão
dos Descobrimentos) make the expedition more than worthwhile.
The Belém Tower is an almost unbelievably ornate building with a
large gun-platform, erected in the middle of the harbour in 1515.
Today it stands up against the shore because the contours have

Belém's decorative Manueline Tower

changed. To get the best view of it you need to see it from the
water, and you can do this by taking one of the boat excursions
that show you the whole of Lisbon's port.

The Jerónimos Monastery (Mosteiro dos Jerónimos: also called
the Hieronymite Monastery) was started in 1502. It is one of the
finest examples of Manueline design and contains also some
Plateresque elements. Buildings added during the 19th century
unfortunately seem rather out of place. While the church, dedicated to St Mary, is impressive, the magnificently ornate cloisters
are completely overwhelming. The National Archaeological and
Ethnographic Museum (Museu Nacional de Arqueologia e
Etnografia) occupies one of the monastery's wings.

The National Museum of Ancient Art lies a little less than half-
way between Black Horse Square and Belém, and can be visited
on either the outward or the return journey. Its most famous
painting is the polyptych of the Adoration of St Vincent by Nuno
Gonçalves, painted in the mid-15th century. The museum contains
gold and silver plate as well as paintings.

Of Lisbon's remaining famous sights, the 25 April Bridge and the
view it provides as you approach the town, together with the
enormous, soaring modern Christ in Majesty that you see to your
left, cannot be omitted. And there are the beautiful Botanical
Gardens on the Avenida da Liberdade, the park just beyond the
Marquis of Pombal Square, the Cold Greenhouse (Estuga Fria)—
a park with a magnificent view over the town and the river; in
addition to many other museums, churches and gardens.

But even if you look at none of Lisbon's special sights you will
still find it an extraordinarily pleasant place to be in. Merely
walking through the streets—whether old or new—sitting in the
gardens, taking boat trips on the river, enjoying the restaurants
and nightspots—including the 'fado restaurants' (see p. 71)—is
occupation enough. All manner of organised excursions are
provided by local travel agents. You can easily and profitably
make Lisbon a base for visiting as far afield as Setúbal to the
south, and Batalha, Alcobaça, Fátima, Coimbra, Obidos, and
many other towns to the north, to say nothing of Estoril, Cascais,
and Sintra, much closer at hand.

Travelling by public transport to or from Lisbon presents a few
problems (see p. 10). It is well worth the effort of collecting a free
map from the Turismo office.

Albufeira

Albufeira today is a popular small coastal holiday town in the
central Algarve. Its picturesque, white-painted centre, perched on

the headland (pierced by a tunnel) which separates the Bathers'
and Fishermen's Beaches, has been occupied for over 2000 years
by Greeks, Romans, Moors, and Portuguese in succession. Apart
from nightclubs, restaurants, bars, boutiques, and hotels (some on
beaches to the east of the town), local colour and bargains are
provided by the daily fruit and vegetable market, at its best early
on Sunday, and the daily fish market, where catches brought in by
the gaily-painted boats are sold. Albufeira is also the centre for
the Clube Praia da Oura and other smaller residential and holiday
developments. Good riding can be enjoyed at one of these, the
Quinta da Saudade, 10 km along the side road to Pera.

Alcobaça

A quiet commercial country town, set among vast fruit orchards
about 60 miles north of Lisbon in a region which also produces
attractive pottery, Alcobaça is world-famous for its magnificent
Santa Maria Monastery. Building, by Cistercian monks, began in
1178 in fulfilment of a vow made by King Afonso I after his
capture of Santarém from the Moors in 1147. Additions and
alterations continued up to the 18th century.

The church has been restored to reveal its original clean lines and
spaciousness. The adjacent Cloister of Silence (14th century with
16th-century upper storey) is also impressive in its simplicity.
Beyond the cloister one can visit the monks' quarters.

The church's transepts contain the magnificently carved tombs of
King Pedro I and his Castilian wife Inês de Castro, whom he had
married secretly in 1345, while still Crown Prince, on the death of
his first wife, Princess Constanza of Castile. King Afonso IV,
Pedro's father, fearing Castilian influence and not knowing of the
marriage, banished her from the Portuguese court. When Pedro
continued to visit her in Coimbra she was murdered. Pedro
rebelled against his father and two years later became king. He
had the hearts of his wife's murderers torn from their living bodies
and brought to him. Six years after Inês's death, her body, then
buried in Coimbra, was exhumed and crowned and the court
forced to pay homage to the decomposing corpse.

A fine terracotta group depicting the death of St Bernard stands
in the south transept near King Pedro's tomb. It was modelled by
monks in the 17th century.

The Manueline doors leading from the spacious ambulatory
beyond the chancel into the sacristy are also specially notable.
The Hall of the Kings (Sála dos Reis), immediately left of the
church's main entrance, contains 18th-century statues of all
Portugal's kings in contemporary costume, together with a
number of azulejos (see p. 33).

Alcobaça can be visited during a long day's excursion from
Lisbon, Estoril, or Cascais.

Almancil (or Almansil) See Quarteira

Alvor and Montes de Alvor See Portimão.

Amarante

Amarante is a pleasant small northern town set among the
mountains and vineyards of the Douro region. The wooden
balconies and iron window-grilles of the 17th to 18th-century
houses give the town a very attractive appearance.

Armacao de Pera

This striking, completely modern Algarve resort, reached by a side
road from the old village of Pera just west of Albufeira, has one of
the Algarve's pleasantest and safest sandy beaches, set in a small
bay ringed by low hills.

Arrábida, Serra da

West of Setúbal, barely 40 km south of Lisbon, the Serra da
Arrábida rises suddenly along the coast towards Cape Espichel out
of an almost completely flat plain. Reaching heights of 500 m
(1600 feet) in places, it slopes steeply to the sea but less sharply
to the north. Towards the sea the slopes are covered with arbutus,
myrtle, and other Mediterranean shrubs, with pines, cypresses, and
a mass of different trees above them. Vineyards, olive groves, and
fruit trees cover the northern slopes.

Aveiro

The old town of Aveiro, busy now, lies in a landscape you do not
expect to find in Portugal—a completely flat expanse of salt
marshes, saltwater lagoons, sandbars, and canals. Outside the
town, centuries-old saltpans still produce high-quality sea-salt, rice
is extensively grown, and cattle are grazed on rich marshlands.
It possesses also large-scale canneries. For visitors, however, the
waterways surrounding the town and the vast sandy beaches 8 km
to the west are the chief attraction. The former Convent of Jesus
has been made into an interesting regional museum. Aveiro is at its
best during the March feira, when *moliceiros* (local boats) sail down
the City Canal.

Barcelos

The colourful little inland town of Barcelos, close to the coast
between Viana do Castelo and Oporto, is famous for its cock, sold
as a good luck emblem throughout Portugal. The story goes that a
pilgrim making his way towards Santiago de Compostela was
convicted of theft in Barcelos. Condemned to die but knowing

himself innocent he declared that the cock which the judge was
about to eat would stand up and crow to prove him right. It did,
and in gratitude the pilgrim presented the town with a carved and
decorated cock which can be seen in Barcelos' archaeological museum.

Batalha

About 120 km north of Lisbon, on the N1, you can see, rising from
a small valley, the forest of pinnacles, buttresses, and turrets of
the magnificent monastery of Batalha. It was built by João I in
fulfilment of a vow he made before the battle of Aljubarrota,
fought against the Castilian claimant to the Portuguese throne in
1385. The monastery took over 150 years to build so that it is a
mixture of different styles, all of which, however, blend extremely
harmoniously.

The church is a magnificent soaring Gothic structure, with the later
Founders' Chapel, to the right of the main entrance, designed in
Flamboyant. The Royal Cloister north of the church is a very
striking mixture of Gothic and ornate Manueline. Leading off the
cloister, the Chapter House with its superb vaulting—almost 20 m
(66 feet) without intermediate supports—contains the shrine of the
Portuguese Unknown Soldier.

The Founders' Chapel is interesting to both Portuguese and British
visitors: in it lies the beautiful joint tomb of João I and his queen,
Philippa, daughter of John of Gaunt. She and her husband
founded the royal line that ruled Portugal till modern times. Their
children, including Prince Henry the Navigator, are also buried here.
The precinct around Batalha Monastery has numerous shops selling
the pottery for which Estremadura province is famous. But the lack
of shade can be trying.

Beja

Beja is a busy country town of white houses and new flats standing
on a hill that rises a little above the Alentejo plateau. It is the capital'
of Lower Alentejo. Originally a Roman city, it was occupied for
four centuries by Moors before becoming a fortress town designed
to repel attacks from Spain. You can still visit the 13th-century
castle. The 15th-century former Convent of the Conception today
houses the regional museum.

Berlenga Island

Tiny Berlenga Island lies 12 km off the coast north of Lisbon and
is reached in about an hour by regular boat services from Peniche.
Its granite coastline is surrounded by caves, reefs, and even smaller
islands. Boats can be hired to make trips round the island. Berlenga
is specially famous for its underwater fishing, and possesses a
simple pousada.

Braga

Important since Roman times, Braga is a main centre of the
modern Minho province. It is an inland town, built on hills and
famous on three counts: for fine ecclesiastical architecture; for its
celebration of the Feast of St John the Baptist on June 23rd and
24th each year; and for its weekly Tuesday market, at which local
craftsmen's products can be bought.

The Cathedral contains architecture of every period from the 12th
to 18th centuries. The Treasury is divided into two parts, one
containing mainly 18th-century church vestments, and the other a
notable collection of 16th-century azulejos. Amongst the chapels,
one contains fine 17th-century azulejos, and another 14th-century
wall paintings in Mudéjar style. Small admission charges are made
for each part of the Treasury, and collectively for the chapels.

The former Episcopal Palace (Antigo Paço Episcopal), another
notable building, dates from the 14th, 16th, and 18th centuries,
and contains one of Portugal's richest libraries, with documents
going back to the 9th century. There are several other churches
and buildings in Braga of architectural interest, many with azulejos.

Bragança

Old Bragança, the walled administrative centre of the remote
north-eastern province of Trás-os-Montes, boasts Portugal's
oldest town hall (12th-century), built to a pentagonal ground-plan;
a 12th-century castle which dominates the old town and provides
superb views from its keep; and a highly decorated pillory. It is
680 m above sea level, and the modern town is located on lower
ground.

Bussaco

Bussaco (Buçaco in Portuguese) is famous for its mountain forest
and for Wellington's victory over Napoleonic troops in 1810. The
forest has been notable since the 6th century, when Benedictine
monks established a hermitage among the original oaks and pines.
They tended the trees carefully, and when the Carmelites built a
monastery on the site of the present hotel in 1628 they planted
new varieties that included maple, cedars, laurels, amongst others.
In 1834, when the religious orders were banned in Portugal, the
government took over the forest and introduced even more varied
planting. Today at Bussaco you can see 400 varieties of native
trees and about 300 exotic species. Eucalyptus, pine, oak, monkey-
puzzle trees, cedars, thuyas, oriental spruces, sequoias, Japanese
camphor trees, and a great deal more flourish here. Bussaco lies
about 30 km north of Coimbra by road, and possesses a hotel

Caldas da Rainha

This quiet little spa town—'the Queen's Spa'—took its name from João II's queen in 1484. Seeing country people bathing in foul-smelling pools at the roadside, she stopped, tried them for herself, and was so pleased with the results that she stayed on. Later she founded a hospital and a church in the town and ordered a large park to be laid out. The Spa Park is still delightful and has a good campsite.

Caldas is a pleasant touring base for the region north of Lisbon.

Cape St Vincent See Sagres.

Carcavelos See Estoril.

Cascais

The ancient fishing port of Cascais, at the foot of the Sintra hills just west of Lisbon, began its transformation into the popular resort it is today in the summer of 1870, when the court moved there for the first time. It stands on a wide bay with a beautiful sandy beach. Inland, mountains slope sharply up from the town, providing cooling breezes in summer. A former royal palace, then one of the President's residences, stands on the promontory to the south-west. A good entertainment and excursion centre.

The stretch of coast running west from Lisbon, on which Cascais, Estoril and other resorts stands, is called the Costa do Sol.

Chaves

This charming hillside town, once a frontier fortress, climbs from the Roman bridge over the Tâmega up to the town square. It provides a delightful welcome to Portugal, 10 km from the Spanish frontier by the N2.

Coimbra

The medieval city centre of Coimbra, Portugal's third largest city, rises in tiers on a steep hill beside the River Mondego. Coimbra was Portugal's first capital and from 1308 has been the home of one of Europe's oldest universities. The old town is picturesque, with narrow winding streets and numerous fine buildings, and occupies a special place in the history and affections of the Portuguese people. During the university terms the presence of several thousand students, wearing black gowns and coloured faculty ribbons—the university teachers also wear special caps— gives the town an even more romantic appearance. Mournful *fados,* different in style from those traditional to Lisbon, are sung in Coimbra by the students. Coimbra has plenty of hotels and restaurants and is a good centre for visiting the three Beira provinces.

Most places of interest are concentrated in the old town and in the newer suburb on the other side of the River Mondego, close to the wide Ponte Santa Clara. To visit the old town first, start in the large triangular 'square' opposite the bridge's end, and walk away from the river till you see on your right the 12th-century Almedina Gate. Turn through it and then keep round left past the Sub Ripas and Arco mansions, both private residences. The first was built in Manueline style early in the 16th century; the second has a fine Renaissance courtyard. Turn right a little past the two houses and then right again up the Rua dos Coutinhos till you come to the Old Cathedral (Sé), a fortress-like building, except for its decorated north door, added later and subsequently badly damaged. The Cathedral was, in fact, erected as a fortress in the mid-12th century when Portugal was still busily fighting the Moors, but it now shows traces of every style of architecture from Romanesque onwards, including Gothic, Baroque, and Mudéjar.

Beyond the Cathedral the former Bishop's Palace now houses the Machado de Castro art museum. This displays porcelain, sculpture, paintings, jewellery, and ecclesiastical plate.

Past the museum, the Rua Sá de Miranda brings you into the main university area. The Old University lies further along to your right. The Old University's library (ring for admission), built in 1724 is a fine piece of Baroque architecture, with ceilings painted in false perspective. Its Manueline chapel is specially famous for the highly decorated door and its fine 17th-century azulejos.

The Monastery of the Holy Cross (Mosteiro de Santa Cruz) lies about 200 m north of the Almedina Gate (continue along the Rua Ferreira Borges leading from the Ponte Santa Clara), and dates from the 16th century. The interior contains much fine architecture. The cloister is a beautiful example of Manueline design.

On the Mondego's other bank you can visit the Old Convent of St Clare (Santa Clara a Velha), where Inês de Castro's body (see Alcobaça) was buried till its transfer to Alcobaça; and also the New Convent of St Clare (Santa Clara a Nova) with its fine Baroque church which contains the 14th-century tomb of Queen St Isabel. The Park of Tears (Quinta das Lagrimas), a small and rather lovely wooded area where Inês de Castro is said to have been murdered, lies about 500 m down the road towards Lisbon. Between them, in very different vein, stands Children's Portugal (Portugal dos Pequenitos), a delightful park containing models of many of Portugal's main historic monuments as well as models of typical houses both from the country itself and from Portugal's overseas territories.

Popular short excursions from Coimbra take visitors to Bussaco Forest (above), and the Roman remains at Conimbriga (see below).

Conimbriga

The remains of Roman Conimbriga, 15 km south-west of
Coimbra, are impressive and give a comprehensive idea of the town
as it was in about the 4th century AD. The site was occupied by
Celts during the Iron Age. The Roman town was captured by
barbarian invaders in AD 468, and lost its importance after the
foundation of modern Coimbra.

Douro Valley

Both the Douro Valley itself and the long vine-covered mountain
slopes stretching for many miles on either side of the river are
notably colourful and picturesque. The area through which the
lower river runs down to the sea at Oporto, from just above
Resende, is noted for the light sparkling white vinho verde ('green
wine') made from grapes that never mature fully. Port wine comes
from grapes grown in the upper valley, stretching as far as the
Spanish frontier (see Oporto).

While the whole region is exceptionally beautiful and most side
roads well worth exploring, one drive is particularly popular, and
takes visitors along the left (southern) bank from Souselo to
Pinhão, by the N222, and then northward to Vila Real, with a call
en route at the Mateus estate near Vila Real, famous throughout
Europe for its rosé wine.

Elvas

Only a few miles from the Spanish frontier and the Spanish
fortress town of Badajoz, Elvas is famous throughout Portugal
chiefly for its superb sugar plums. It deserves, however, to be far
more widely known, both for its magnificent fortifications—an
excellent and impressive example of 17th-century military architecture—and for the beauty of its old white houses, narrow streets,
and charming squares. If you have a car it is well worth driving
round the ramparts. On the way you will see an aqueduct, begun
in the 15th century, which still carries water to the town.

Go into the town from the south and make for the archway (Arco
do Relogio). Go through this into the Praça de Sancho II. The
former Town Hall stands on one side and the former Cathedral on
the other. A street on the right of the cathedral leads to another
delightful square, the Largo Santa Clara, where you can see a fine
example of one of Portugal's many 16th-century pillories, a 16th-
century Renaissance church containing some specially attractive
17th-century azulejos, and also remains of the original 10th-
century Moorish fortifications. If you continue uphill you come to
the Castle. Built originally by the Moors, it was altered and
strengthened in the 14th-16th centuries. A wonderful view of the

town and the surrounding countryside can be had from the ramparts. There is a state pousada in the town.

Espinho See Porto.

Estoril

Estoril on the Costa do Sol, reached in under half-an-hour from Lisbon by fast electric train, is Portugal's largest and most fashionable coast resort. The town, looking across the bay to Cascais, 3 km away, is elegantly and attractively built, and its park contains a wealth of exotic tropical plants. Estoril provides almost everything that holidaymakers could wish for—including good hotels and restaurants, and plentiful excursions to places like Lisbon, Sintra, Cascais, Obidos, Batalha, and Carcavelos, a more modest resort, 7 km from Estoril towards Lisbon. The climate is mild in winter, and in summer the heat is tempered by breezes from the mountains.

The fashionable Estoril seafront

Estrela, Serra da

Of all of Portugal's innumerable mountain chains, the Serra da Estrela is the most grandiose and impressive. 60 km long and 30 wide, rising to a height of nearly 2000 m (over 6,500 feet), it consists mostly of vast treeless plateaux, boulder-strewn cliff-like slopes, and frighteningly deep gorges. The rebuilt road between Seia and Covilhã is particularly impressive. It passes close by Torre, the range's highest peak. A modern ski resort is taking shape at Penhas da Saude, which you pass on this route. Simple accommodation is available at both Seia and Covilhã.

Estremoz

Estremoz, another of the Upper Alentejo's beautiful fortified
towns, lies about 50 km further from Elvas on the main road
running from Badajoz in Spain through Elvas to Lisbon. Dominated by its medieval castle and 17th-century ramparts, Estremoz is
today famous for the pottery manufactured there, and also for its
figurines. Scores of stalls sell them at the market held on Saturdays.

A good regional museum stands in the main square known as the
Rossio, with two pillories close by. From here you can walk into
the old town and up to the Castle and King Dinis I's palace, now
a pousada. The castle chapel contains lovely azulejos that tell the
story of Queen St Isabel of Aragon, King Dinis's wife. St Mary's
Church, which is square, formed part of the original citadel.

Evora

Evora, some 30 miles south-west of Estremoz, is the largest and
most famous of all the Alentejo's famous fortified towns. The city
walls are vast and impressive. Many of the old town's cobbled
streets are as narrow and winding as those you find in any
Moorish medina, though the houses are often beautifully built and
adorned with their former owners' coats-of-arms. The Cathedral
(Sé) stands at the top of the hill in the town centre, with the
remains of a Roman temple, dedicated to Diana the goddess of
hunting, at a slightly higher level. There was once a university in
the town.

Roman temple and Cathedral at Evora

A street running south from the cathedral takes you to the famous
Moura Gates Square (Largo das Portas de Moura), where you can
see a delightful Renaissance fountain, some aristocratic houses,
and part of the town's medieval fortifications.

The Rua da Republica, leading to the railway station, contains two
of the town's more interesting churches: the São Francisco, built
in a local version of Gothic-Manueline style and including an
extraordinary ossuary chapel with hundreds of monks' skeletons
set into the wall; and the São Bras Hermitage, a Gothic-Mudejar
building dating from 1480.

These are only the outstanding items, suitable for a quick visit.
Evora deserves a longer stay and more detailed exploration. The
Turismo office provides excellent town plans free. It is also a good
centre from which to explore the unusual Upper Alentejo region
with its many fortified towns, such as Elvas, Estremoz, and
Evoramonte, to name a few.

Faro

A busy commercial and fishing centre in the centre of the Algarve
coast, Faro is the province's modern capital, as well as an important tourist centre. Though separated from the open sea by a large
lagoon bounded by sandbars, Faro's port is still lively and busy.
The international airport serving the whole Algarve lies 4 km west
of the town.

Faro was an important city when it was captured from the Moors
in 1249. Two hundred years later its Jewish community printed
Portugal's first books. The town was sacked by British naval forces
in 1596, during the period when Portugal formed part of Spain. It
was damaged by an earthquake in 1722, and the great 'quake of
1755 reduced it to ruins once again. Bishop Dom Francisco
Gomes, commemorated by an obelisk in the square close to the
harbour named after him, fought hard for its reconstruction and is
largely responsible for the town's present prosperity.

The tiny original town lies south of the harbour. Though the
ramparts have disappeared their position can be clearly seen in the
ring of houses surrounding the area. The Cathedral, containing
notable azulejos, occupies the old town's central point, with a
square lined with orange trees to one side. An entertaining
Maritime Museum (Museu Maritimo) lies off one side of the square.
Models of various types of fishing boats form its chief attraction.

In the busy new town to the north the Rua de Santo António
contains a number of fashionable boutiques and shops. The small
Ethnological Museum has exhibits that deal very effectively with
all the Algarve's traditional handicrafts and everyday life.

At the town's main beach area, Praia de Faro, you can enjoy
surfing on the sandbar's open side, as well as water-skiing in the
lagoon's calmer waters.

Faro is a good yachting centre. Boats, however, cannot be hired,
though excursions can be arranged with local fishermen, including
fishing expeditions. Coach excursions are run to all places of
interest along the coast on either side of Faro and there are
frequent air, rail, and coach connections with Lisbon.

Fátima

Twenty km from Batalha and about 150 from Lisbon, this little
town's world-wide fame is derived from remarkable events that
occurred in May 1917. Three local children, watching their parents'
sheep grazing a mile from the village, had a vision of a beautiful
lady who promised she would come back on the 13th of each
month until October, when she would reveal who she was. When
news of the children's story reached the Lisbon papers, every sort
of pressure was put on them by the anti-clerical authorities of the
time, but they stuck unshakeably to their original account. Their
firmness created such an impression that on October 12th a crowd
of over 70,000 people gathered at Fátima, hoping to see the vision
for themselves.

On the morning of the 13th the weather was terrible. The sky was
covered with thick cloud, and it rained heavily. No one except the
eldest of the children, Lucia, saw the vision, but everyone saw the
sun suddenly appear through the clouds and seem to revolve
like a ball of fire. Lucia said that the vision had revealed itself as
Our Lady of the Rosary and had ordered a chapel to be built on
the spot, where the people of the world could come to do penance
for their terrible sin—taken as a reference to World War I. The
two younger children died in the influenza epidemic of 1919-20 and
are buried in the basilica built in accordance with the vision's
command. Lucia became a nun and still lives in a convent near
Coimbra. The events were formally recognised as miraculous by
the Roman Catholic church authorities in 1930, and Fátima
became an official place of pilgrimage.

On the 12th of every month from May to October, huge numbers
of pilgrims assemble and go in procession along the wide esplanade
leading to the basilica with its 65 m-high tower. Masses are
celebrated inside and outside the basilica, at which tens of
thousands of people receive Communion together. Many who are
sick also come to be healed. Apart from the basilica and the
esplanade leading to it, a shrine near the evergreen oak in which
the vision appeared—the present tree is a replacement—contains a
statue of the Virgin. The spot where a spring burst suddenly from

the ground, on the occasion of the vision's final appearance, is
marked by a column.

As a town, Fátima has no great distinction. There are, of course,
plenty of places where visitors can be accommodated.

Figueira da Foz

A huge beach of fine white sand lines Figueira Bay at the mouth
of the River Mondego, about 45 km west of Coimbra. The new
part of the town, to the west, is one of the seaside resorts most
popular with Portuguese holidaymakers and offers a wide choice
of leisure occupations, sport, and entertainment. The town's
celebration of the Feast of St John the Baptist on June 23rd-24th is a
very colourful occasion.

Figueira's eastern half is still devoted largely to the centuries-old
sardine and cod-fishing industries, and to shipyards. A range of
hills to the north, the Serra da Bõa Viagem, provides a wonderful
view of the town and of the saltmarshes to the south from its
highest point. A circular drive, going westward towards Cape
Mondego (Cabo Mondego), and then inland towards the view-
point, takes you past the picturesque little fishing village of
Buarcos.

Figueira is a good centre from which to visit Coimbra, Fátima,
Aveiro, Batalha, Alcobaça, etc. Historians know it as the place
where Wellington landed his first troops in August 1808, after the
fort which still overlooks Figueira Bay had been captured by
Coimbra students.

Guarda

Guarda, 54 km from Spain on the main road leading eastward
from Viseu and Coimbra, is Portugal's highest town—1040 m
(over 3,400 feet) above sea level on one of the Serra da Estrela's
foothills. Once it was the main fortress of the province of Beira
Alta. Today it is an administrative centre and mountain resort.
The 14th to 18th-century Cathedral has some attractive corners.
Aristocratic houses ornamented with former owners' coats-of-arms
can be seen in the Cathedral square and in Rua do Dom Luis I
leading off it.

Guimarães

Guimarães is an inland town not far from the coast in the Minho
province. Founded in the 10th century, it consisted originally of
little more than a monastery with a defensive tower. Today it is a
flourishing commercial centre whose industries include textiles,
tanning, jewellery-making, pottery, embroidery, the manufacture
of cutlery and kitchenware, and the carving of the highly decorative wooden yokes that you see on the necks of all the oxen

pulling carts in the Minho region. Portugal's first king was born at Guimarães in about 1112. The writer Gil Vicente was born in the town in 1470.

The enormously tall 10th-century tower still dominates the town that has grown around it. It stands at the top of a hill whose slopes have been turned into a pleasant public park with the Dukes' Palace (Paço dos Duques) to the south, and the old town's centre beyond it. The long Largo da Republica do Brasil contains a fine mosaic pavement, such as is found in many Portuguese towns, and is surrounded by picturesque old houses.

The Castle was thoroughly restored in 1940. The views from it are magnificent. A small Romanesque chapel, where Portugal's first king was baptised, stands near the Castle. The Palace of the Dukes of Bragança, usually known as the Paço dos Duques, is only a little further away. It is a lavishly decorated 15th-century house, open to the public, and containing notable tapestries, paintings, and furniture. There are many other notable old buildings.

Lagoa

Lagoa, an attractive inland Algarve town between Portimão and Albufeira, is known chiefly as a wine-producing centre, though it also offers a strategically-situated motel.

Lagos

Lagos, near the western end of the Algarve coast, lies on a wide estuary, well sheltered from Atlantic gales by the Ponta da Piedade promontory. It is an extremely colourful small town, whose strong fortifications still surround the central area. A tiny 15th-century fort that once protected the harbour, still filled with colourful fishing vessels, is linked to the land by a drawbridge.

Lagos, today, is an important fishing centre, with a sizeable canning industry, and is also the centre of a rice-growing region. Historically, it is famous chiefly as the starting point of Prince Henry the Navigator's 15th-century voyages (see p. 30). A statue of Gil Eanes, or Eannes, overlooks the harbour in front of the town's main entrance. He was the first man to sail further south than Cape Bojador, on Africa's west coast, then the known world's limit.

St Anthony's Church (Igreja Santo António), a little beyond the larger church overlooking the harbour, despite its plain facade is filled with extraordinarily exuberant Baroque decoration—the ceiling pointed in false relief and the walls covered with gilded wood-carving.

Modern resort developments for which Lagos serves as a main centre include Luz Bay on the Praia da Luz, about 6 km west; the

Ponta da Piedade, 2 km due south; the Praia de Dona Ana and
Meia Praia to the east; together with new accommodation in the
tiny fishing villages of Burgau and Salema, 4 and 8 km respectively
beyond Luz Bay. But these occupy only six of the many sandy
beaches stretching along the coast on either side of Lagos.

Lamego

Small town in pleasant countryside 40 km south of Vila Real,
famous for its baroque sanctury reached by a long, magnificently
balustraded stone staircase.

Leiria

Roughly 130 km north of Lisbon on the main Oporto road (N1),
Leiria is a pretty country town on the River Liz. Its two halves
are connected by a Roman bridge, still in use. Both the town and
the surrounding region are dominated by a great castle, open to
the public, started in 1135 by Afonso I, Portugal's first king, on a
plateau high above the town. The view from its battlements
extends seawards over the great forest planted by King Dinis I
in the 13th century to prevent winter gales spreading sand inland.
Leira today is famous for its handicrafts and its folklore. Many
women still wear their traditional costume. The region's folk-
dancing can be seen at its best during Leiria's annual fair (end of
March-early April).

Loulé

Loulé is a busy inland commercial and manufacturing town in the
central Algarve, typical in style, and noted for its Carnival and
Almond Gatherers' Fair that starts each year on the Saturday
before Shrove Tuesday and lasts 4 days.

Mafra

The plateau town of Mafra, 45 km north of Lisbon, and half-
way between Sintra and Torres Vedras (see below), has grown up
beside an enormous monastery whose construction was ordered
in 1717 by King João V. The building was in thanksgiving for the
birth of a daughter, and is on an extraordinarily lavish scale. It
covers 4 hectares (10 acres). Building materials for it came from
Portugal, Belgium, France, Italy, Holland, and Brazil. 50,000 men
worked on it, and construction lasted 13 years. Its frontage of
220 m (over 260 yards) is greater even than that of the famous
El Escorial monastery near Madrid, built 1563-84, which, it is said,
Mafra was intended to rival. With so many foreign architects and
artists gathered in Mafra for the monastery's construction, King
João took the opportunity to found there a school of sculpture,
whose teachers, then and later, included many famous artists
whose works can be seen throughout Portugal.

You can visit the superb marble basilica that forms the central point

in the frontage, and also parts of the former palace and monastery.
Notable features in the basilica include the jasper and marble
altarpieces and the superb, lofty pink and white marble cupola.
In the palace and monastery you can see the monks' cells, their
kitchens, hospital, and pharmacy, the royal apartments, one of the
sculpture studios, and the magnificent library housed in a vast
Baroque gallery containing some 35,000 volumes.

Miranda do Douro

Miranda do Douro is perched picturesquely above a sheer drop
to the River Douro and the Spanish frontier in Portugal's remotest
north-eastern corner. It is famous for its traditional Pauliteiros
sword dance, best seen at the annual *romaria* to the shrine of Our
Lady of Nazo (*Nossa Senhora de Nazo*) at the village of Povoa,
11 km north of Miranda, on September 7th and 8th.

Monchique

The hills which separate the Algarve and Alentejo provinces reach
their highest point—902 m, almost 3000 feet— at Mount Fóia in
the Serra de Monchique in the western Algarve. The road running
north from Portimão or Silves through carobs, arbutus, and wild
rhododendrons, as well as fields of cotton and sugar, is particularly
attractive; while the view from the heights extends to Portimão,
Lagos, and Cape St Vincent. The route to Fóia takes you through
the small spa of Caldas de Monchique and the village of
Monchique, notable only for the unexpectedly ornate Manueline
doorway of the parish church.

Monte Gordo

Once a prosperous small fishing village on the Algarve coast's
eastern end, beside the mouth of the River Guadiana, Monte
Gordo has developed into a large and important modern coast
resort, thanks mainly to its enormous beach of fine white sand and
the pines that cover large areas of the surrounding countryside.
The resort can offer almost all the amenities for which the Algarve
coast is famous (see pp. 33 and 35).

Nazaré

Nazaré, one of Portugal's and Europe's most famous and most
photographed fishing ports, lies about 120 km north of Lisbon in a
cliff-bound bay on the Estremadura coast. It owes its fame partly
to its position but mainly to the colourful activities of the fishermen.
Both men and women wear mainly black woollen garments.
Their boats are painted with brilliant colours in designs that
sometimes recall the themes of ancient magic. With their high
prows and sterns, designed to protect them against being over-
whelmed by the steep Atlantic rollers, they look as though they

may well have been derived from the Phoenicians—the first, as far
as we know, to settle in Nazaré. The beach has no protecting
breakwater or sheltered harbour and launching the boats into the
Atlantic surf, for all the regularity with which it is accomplished,
invariably strikes visitors as a near-miraculous feat. Hauling the
boats back on shore when they return with their catches—oxen
are still used—is no less spectacular. Everyone within reach,
including tourists (if they want the locals' goodwill) helps. A siren
sounds the starting signal. And once the catch is safely ashore the
women carry vast loads of fish on their heads to the fish market—
though much of the catch nowadays goes to the town's flourishing
canneries.

The upper town, the Sítio (O Sítio), most easily reached from the
beach by a funicular, is perched on the top of one of Portugal's
highest cliffs, some 110 m (over 350 feet) above the sea. The
northern part of the lower town, known as A Praia (The Beach),
contains the narrow streets and tiny houses of the fishermen's
quarter, while the new town, called Pederneira, stretches southwards
beside the gigantic sandy beach. The best view of the town and its
beach is the one from the belvedere built into the Sítio's cliffside.

With its fine beach (though poor bathing), Nazaré has naturally
become a holiday resort popular with Portuguese and discerning
foreign visitors. Riding, tennis, and boat excursions are available.

Obidos

Obidos is an enchanting, tiny, medieval walled town filled with
white-painted houses. It is situated on an inland hilltop about 45
km south of Nazaré. The walls date from the time of the

Obidos: Church of Santa Maria in the main square

Moorish occupation, but were extended by the Portuguese in the 12th, 13th, and 16th centuries, following the capture of the town in 1148. In recent years a lot of restoration work has been done, and the tiny town now earns its living purely from tourism. But that does not prevent it being one of Europe's most charming and worthwhile tourist traps. The winding streets, the ring of ancient ramparts, and the town's churches that date from the 15th century on, are well set off by flowers that grow everywhere in great profusion.

King Dinis I visited Obidos in 1228, accompanied by his wife, Queen St Isabel. She was so enchanted by the little town that the King gave it to her as a present. Subsequent Portuguese kings continued the tradition of presenting Obidos to their Queens until as late as 1833. In the 16th century the castle at the highest point of the town became a royal residence. More recently it was transformed into a delightful pousada that makes a wonderful touring base—provided you do not mind its rather steep medieval stairs.

Obidos is excellently placed for car trips to all the main places of interest in Estremadura province, and features in many coach excursions from Lisbon, Estoril, Cascais, etc.

Olhão

A busy little sardine-fishing and canning port on the Algarve coast some 8 km east of Faro, Olhão is known to visitors mainly as a picturesque town of innumerable white and blue cube-shaped houses. Unfortunately they are being increasingly hidden from sight by taller—and duller—modern buildings. Olhão is a minor resort as well as a fishing port. Like Faro it lies on a lagoon. Its beach, on the sandbar enclosing the lagoon, is reached by ferry.

Oporto

The town's name, usually written plain Porto ('Port') in modern Portuguese (O Porto means 'The Port'), derives from the twin Roman towns of Portus and Cale which once stood on opposite shores of the River Douro. Portus-Cale or Portucale, as the base from which the Moorish invaders were driven out, also gave its name to the modern country.

Later in history, Oporto fitted out the expedition of Prince Henry the Navigator which captured the town of Ceuta on the Moroccan Mediterranean coast, in 1415—the start of Portugal's great era of discovery and conquest. The requisitioning of all the local cattle to feed the troops had a curious result—if a long-standing tradition can be believed. The fighting men took all the meat, and the local people, left with the offal, developed a taste for tripe. *Tripas á modo do Porto*—tripe cooked the Oporto way—is still a popular dish and the people of the town are still referred to by other Portuguese as *tripeiros* ('tripe-eaters').

Oporto today, with some 350,000 inhabitants, ranks as Portugal's second city. It occupies a lovely site on hills sloping down to the Douro's northern bank a few miles before the river joins the sea. In former times the wide Douro formed something of a barrier to communications with the country to its north. Today Oporto is linked to the opposite shore by three notable bridges. The oldest and furthest upstream, the Dona Maria Pia railway bridge, was built entirely of cast iron in 1877 by the French engineer Eiffel, of Eiffel Tower fame. The second, the Dom Luis I road bridge, ingeniously serves both upper and lower town levels on both banks of the river by carrying two roads over the water. The third, the Arrábida road bridge furthest downstream, carries the modern motorway across the river in a single concrete span of almost 270 m (295 yards)—a world record at the time of its construction in 1953.

Both road bridges provide interesting views as you approach the town. The Dom Luis I bridge leads directly into the old town centre, with most of the places of interest to the left as you arrive. In an area little more than 800 m (about half-a-mile) square you can see the old city's picturesque alleys leading up to the Cathedral Square, the Cathedral itself with the former Bishop's Palace beside it, Prince Henry the Navigator's House, the Stock Exchange (containing a mock-Moorish hall), the Ethnographic Museum, the São Francisco Church with its overpoweringly magnificent Baroque interior, the so-called 'English Factory'—now serving as a club for British wine-merchants, and the Clérigos church's lofty tower.

The Cathedral began its existence as a 12th-century fortress church. Its severe exterior gives little hint of the 16th to 17th-century splendour inside. The 14th-century cloisters adjoining it to the south, are decorated with 18th-century azulejos illustrating the life of the Virgin and scenes from the Roman poet Ovid's *Metamorphoses*—a juxtaposition which probably seemed quite normal at the time.

The main road that the Dom Luis I bridge runs into leads north into the enormous double avenue composed of the Praça da Liberdade, the Avenida dos Aliados, and the Praça do Municipio, with a very grand Town Hall at its end (the Turismo office at pavement level on the right-hand corner provides free maps and information). The city's main shopping and commercial area is spread around this central space.

Avenida dos Aliados, Oporto

To the British, Oporto is more or less synonymous with port wine. However, the wineries are all on the Douro's other bank, in the suburb of Vila Nova de Gaia. They all keep open house to visitors except on Sundays and public holidays and, in some cases, Saturday afternoons. Here you will be taken round and shown the immense vats in which the maturing process begins. Initial fermentation and the addition of the brandy which puts a halt to it, retaining some of the grape's natural sugar, takes place before the wine comes down the Douro in barges to Vila Nova. For over 200 years the British have been the main customers for dessert, or tawny, port—the Portuguese and others drink also the dry white port as an aperitif—and many of the great shipping firms have been controlled by the same Anglo-Portuguese families for a century or more. Free tastings are included.

There is far more to see in Oporto than we have space to describe in detail here. Other museums and ancient churches, for instance, fine parks, the vast new harbour at Leixões nearer the sea, and the lively resort-suburbs of Foz do Douro, south of Leixões, and Matosinhos to its north. Espinho, 16 km south, has a good beach and a golf course.

Peniche

About 25 km west of Obidos, Peniche is Portugal's third most important fishing port, where crayfish, tunny, sardines, and other catches are landed and canned. The town has long been famous for pillow-lace. Peniche is also the embarkation point for the 1-hour journey to Berlenga Island (see above). The Citadel, built to command the approach to the 2-km long Cape Carvoeiro promontory, has retained its 17th-century ramparts almost intact.

Penina See Portimão.

Pombal

Pombal is a small town about 45 km south of Coimbra on the
main road between Lisbon and Oporto. It possesses a castle
originally built in the 12th century by a Grand Master of the
Knights Templar

Portalegre

Only a few km from Marvão, Castelo de Vide, and the Spanish
frontier, Portalegre is an important provincial centre in the Upper
Alentejo. The town became prosperous with the foundation of silk
mills in the 17th century, and many fine houses from this period
can still be seen. A tapestry-weaving factory is situated in the
former Jesuit monastery, and the ramparts surrounding the
original town are still largely intact. Portalegre offers a good
selection of places to stay.

Portimão

Portimão, 20 km east of Lagos, is the Algarve's most picturesque
and busiest fishing port. You get a very good view of the harbour
and the brightly-painted fishing boats from the bridge over the
River Arade, as you come into the town from the east. Portimão
is also quite an important boat-building and fish-canning centre.
Not in itself a resort, it is the base for the large and important
tourist developments at Penina and Torralta to the west, and
serves also the well-established resort of Praia da Rocha (south),
and the growing holiday centre of Praia dos Tres Irmãos.

Penina is noted for its golf courses, its vast and luxurious Golf
Hotel, casino, riding, tennis, and other amenities. Strictly speaking,
its location should be given as Montes de Alvor. Torralta, at Alvor
nearer the coast, already possesses huge numbers of apartments
and villas, together with restaurants, tennis, and riding. The Praia
dos Tres Irmãos lies close to Torralta. For Praia da Rocha see
below.

Póvoa de Varzim

Lying beside a lovely beach of fine white sand about 30 km north
of Oporto, Póvoa de Varzim is a well-established resort that has
grown up beside an ancient fishing port. The fishermen's quarter
with its small houses lies to the south, and the beach opposite it is
almost as busy and colourful as the shore at Nazaré. One main
difference is that the men wear white woollen jerseys embroidered
in varied colours. Collecting seaweed for use as fertiliser is also a
regular foreshore occupation. Apart from its fine beach, the resort
district offers underwater fishing, sea-fishing, and a host of
amenities including bullfighting, and a casino.

Praia da Luz See Lagos.

Praia da Our See Albufeira.

Praia da Rocha

Though administratively a suburb of Portimão, Praia da Rocha is one of the Algarve's best-known resorts whose fine, sandy beach, punctuated by tall clumps of eroded rocks, has appeared on innumerable posters. The town, all newly-built and still expanding, stands on low cliffs overlooking the beach. It provides a full range of holiday facilities.

Quarteira

Quarteira is a small Algarve fishing port, half-way between Albufeira and Faro. The centre of a major holiday area, it serves, together with Almancil, 7 km inland, as a base for three of the Algarve's largest and most important holiday and residential developments—Vilamoura, Vale de Lobo, and Quinta do Lago. All are exceptionally luxurious and laid out among vast expanses of gently rolling land, liberally sprinkled with umbrella pines. All three have golf courses, tennis courts, riding centres, and, of course, good swimming. In addition, Vale de Lobo boasts an extremely luxurious hotel. Vilamoura has the Algarve's first specially-designed marina, 2 golf courses, a casino, several hotels, and much else.

Quelez

Queluz, 13 km west of Lisbon, possesses a former royal palace built between 1758 and 1794 in imitation of Versailles. The throne room is particularly sumptuous, and one of the guardrooms contains azulejos depicting Chinese and Brazilian scenes. The very attractive gardens were laid out in 1762 in imitation of Le Nôtre's style (Versailles's gardens and the original St James's Park in London).

Quinta do Lago See Quarteira.

Sagres

Sagres today is an unimportant village at the extreme western end of the Algarve coast. Its fame comes from the bare, rock-covered bleak promontory, hundreds of feet above sea level, surrounded by sheer drops into the unresting Atlantic which stretches south-west from the village. It was here that Prince Henry established his epoch-making School of Navigation (see p. 30). There is little to see—just the tiny chapel of Our Lady of Grace (Nossa Senhora das Graças), and a low building that has been turned into a Youth Hostel, where a film about Prince Henry and the great discoveries is shown each day (English version 15.30). The windswept site is enormously impressive, with its view of the cliff-lined bay.

Cape St Vincent itself, only 6 km from Sagres, can also be visited from the village. Its associations with British naval history—to say nothing of Robert Browning's poem 'Oh to be in England now that April's there'—make it almost a place of pilgrimage for Britons.

Salema See Lagos.

Santarém

Santarém stands on a hill beside the River Tagus, overlooking the vast plain of the Ribatejo province, whose capital it is. Its name is derived from St Irene, a 7th-century nun. Her body floated ashore at this point after she had been murdered by a monk whose advances she had rejected. The town's recapture from the Moors in 1147 was a vital step in the Christian reconquest of Portugal.

Santarém has been built on a steep hill. Its winding streets are lined with pantiled and tile-hung houses, and its many squares provide an air of spaciousness. It is famous for bullfighting, the Ribatejo bulls being considered Portugal's best.

The city's main sights include the vast square known as the Campo de Sá de Bandeira.

There are several interesting churches in the town.

An archaeological museum with exhibits going back to Moorish times is also housed in a former church, that of São João de Alporão.

Santarém is a possible touring base although it possesses only modest hotels.

Santiago de Cacém

Some 140 km south of Lisbon on the main road to Lagos, Santiago do Cacém is a small town dominated by a 13th-century castle built by the Templars. Sines, one of Portugal's best sea-fishing bases, lies 17 km south-west. Santiago's pousada provides rather simpler accommodation than most State inns.

São Bras de Alportel

São Bras is a small inland Algarve town in the hills 17 km north of Faro on the main road to Lisbon. A pousada with fine views stretching down to the coast stands on the town's highest point.

Sesimbra

Sesimbra is a tiny fishing port 60 km south of Lisbon and about 30 west of Setúbal. It is also something of an international holiday resort, with one four-star hotel and other, more modest accommodation. Sesimbra is famous chiefly for its sea-fishing, its sandy beach, and its fishermen's Festival of Our Lady of the Wounds which takes place every May 3rd-5th, and includes processions, fireworks, and other festivities.

Setúbal

Setúbal, at the other end of the Serra de Arrábida from Sesimbra, lies on the enormously broad Sado estuary. Like Faro in the Algarve, it is famous for the breeding of young oysters. Thousands of tons are shipped every year to France. It is an important industrial area with activities that include cement manufacture, chemicals, car and lorry assembly, and fish canning. Setúbal is also a notable fishing centre with a fleet of some 2000 boats, a major port—Portugal's third busiest—and a flourishing resort. It is known, too, for its muscatel wine and its marmalade. The town has been important for many centuries—the remains of Roman villas can be visited on the Troia promontory across the Sado—and the old centre, with its narrow alleys and small houses, forms a striking contrast to the modern town's broad avenues and spacious houses.

St Philip's Castle, west of the town, was built in 1590 during the Spanish occupation, partly to intimidate the people of Setúbal and partly to prevent an English invasion. The Church of Jesus (Igreja de Jesus), off the broad Avenida 22 de Dezembro running north-wards from the old town's western edge, was built of Arrábida marble in 1491 and contains the earliest examples of Manueline decoration in all Portugal. The chancel pillars and vaulting are outstanding. Adjoining the church, the Municipal Museum (Museu da Cidade) displays a fine collection of 15th and 16th-century Portuguese paintings in the upper galleries, with 16th-century azulejos decorated in Moorish-style geometric designs downstairs.

Setúbal offers tennis, riding, boat excursions, and sea-fishing as well as first-rate swimming. The beaches on the Troia promontory are of particularly fine sand. You reach them by a 20-minute ferry trip from the quay beside the yacht harbour (doca de recreio).

Silves

Once an important port and the capital of the region during the Moorish occupation, when it was known as Xelb, Silves lies a little inland towards the Algarve's western end. In the course of centuries the River Arade, on which the town stands, has silted up so that only tiny vessels can reach it by water today. At the height of its fame and prosperity, however, during the 11th and 12th centuries, Xelb was said to rival even Lisbon in its magnificence. The sandstone walls of the vast Moorish castle rising above the town still recall something of those days of glory. When it was captured by Crusaders and Portuguese, in 1244, this fortress could hold 30,000 men. The vast cistern that guaranteed them a whole year's water supply can still be seen. From the battlements there is a fine view over the hills, woods, and cork factories of the surrounding region. Silves' former Cathedral, built soon after the town was captured by the Crusaders, is simple but beautiful. The many tombs that you see in it are said to contain Crusaders killed in the attack on the town.

Sines See Santiago da Cacém.

Sintra

The name Sintra indicates two interlinked attractions—the extraordinary granite Serra de Sintra, with its wild scenery and many fascinating old buildings, and the little town of Sintra containing the elegant small palace that was a favourite residence of Portugal's kings for some 600 years. The town lies on the northern slopes of the miniature mountain range, about 30 km north-west of Lisbon. The little Serra de Sintra, roughly 10 km long and 5 wide, rising to a maximum height of 530 m (1730 feet), possesses an extraordinary richness and grandeur, due partly to the region's granite ruggedness and partly to its contradictory-seeming dense green vegetation. Every sort of tree and shrub found in northern, Mediterranean, and tropical regions grows wild here—and to a tremendous size. The eucalyptus trees, in particular, are enormously tall. In several places great forests of them sweep down steep hillsides incongruously carpeted with the thick bracken associated with northern climates. Not surprisingly, the Serra de Sintra's beauty has been sung by many poets, including Southey and Byron. In sordid technical terms the scenery is simply a result of the conjunction of Mediterranean-region warmth with rain-carrying clouds coming in from the Atlantic and dropping their moisture on the granite mountain.

A picturesque circular drive from Sintra takes you out past the house called Seteais (Seven Sighs)—where Wellington signed an armistice permitting the French to leave Portugal unharmed in 1808, to the great disappointment of the Portuguese—and then to the little wine town of Colares, and to Almocageme 5 km beyond. On the way you can visit the beautifully landscaped Monserrate Park surrounding a neo-Oriental 18th-century palace. At Almocageme you turn back towards Sintra by the southern road. A turning takes you to a long-deserted Capuchin monastery (Convento dos Capuchos) where you can see the monks' tiny cells cut into the rock and lined with cork. Another steep, rough lane leads up to tiny Peninha chapel, whose interior is lined with 17th-century azulejos. It stands on a hilltop 486 m (almost 1600 feet) above the sea, with magnificent views that include the huge sandy Guincho beach to the south-west. Later you come to the ruins of an ancient Moorish castle spread over several rocky hilltops—you have to walk up from a conveniently-sited car park—with Pena Palace on a neighbouring peak, and its superb vast park containing all manner of rare trees. The Palace itself was built in the 19th century, round a 16th-century monastery, in a jumble of styles. Beyond Pena you tumble steeply back into Sintra down a series of sharp hairpin bends, passing on the way the Estalagem dos Cavaleiros, where Byron planned *Childe Harold*. This whole route, efficiently signposted throughout, takes you up and down densely forested steep mountainsides with continuously changing magnificent views. If you have time for nothing else in Portugal, you should make this tour. A short extension from Colares allows you to visit the beautiful seaside village of Azenhas do Mar, perched on a cliffside.

In Sintra town the chief attraction is the Royal Palace (Paço Real). The building was begun in the 14th century and is dominated by two extraordinarily tall conical chimneys. Every period since the Palace's foundations were laid has left its mark: there are Moorish and Manueline windows, 16th and 17th-century azulejos, a fine Armoury, and a Reading Room whose ceiling is painted with magpies—a king's gibe at gossiping court ladies.

A quick look at Sintra is sometimes included in coach tours from Lisbon that take in also Estoril and Cascais, or with trips from the two latter resorts that go much further afield. But the region deserves much more time than this.

Tavira

Tavira is an ancient town standing a few kilometres from the coast near the Algarve's border with Spain. Its bridge over the River Gilão in the town centre stands on Roman foundations. The ramparts of the fortress above the town go back to Moorish times and allow the visitor to see the fine view over the town. The church of St Mary of the Castle (Santa Maria do Castelo) was originally a mosque. St Paul's Church contains Dutch tiles imported into Portugal in the earliest days of the azulejos craze.

Tavira today is a typically quiet Algarve town. In July and August it becomes a busy centre for tunny fishing, carried out with the aid of huge nets in which the fish, weighing up to a quarter of a ton each, are trapped and then killed by hand.

Tomar

The little town of Tomar lies along the banks of the River Nabão,
20 km east of Fátima and about 40 from Batalha. It is a quiet
spot, with narrow streets and shaded gardens, dominated by a
small wooded hill. On the summit of the hill 12th-century fortifications enclose the beautiful buildings that were formerly the
headquarters of the Order of Christ.

In 1160 a Grand Master of the Knights Templar built a fortified
castle on the hilltop. In 1314, however, the Templars were
disbanded at the Pope's request and, a few years later, King Dinis
I created the purely Portuguese Order of Christ. They took over
the castle at Tomar and in the centuries that followed added
considerably to the Templars' structure, making it one of·
Portugal's outstanding buildings.

Apart from the fortification walls, the monastery's oldest part is
the Templars' Rotunda (Charola), built in the 12th century on the
model of the Church of the Holy Sepulchre that still stands in
Jerusalem's Old City. In shape it is a 16-sided polygon, containing
a two-storeyed octagonal structure supported on columns and
topped by a cupola. The paintings and coloured statues in this
striking building date from the 16th century.

The church nave which the Order of Christ built onto the
Rotunda's western side is notable chiefly for its extraordinarily
exuberant Manueline design, though the doorway into the church
is reminiscent of the Plateresque style seen at its best in Salamanca
and other Spanish cities (see p. 32). The nave's west end opens
directly onto the Renaissance Santa Barbara cloisters, and a spiral
staircase near the doorway leads to the upper gallery and to the
window considered the most astonishing example of Manueline
ornateness in all Portugal. Ropes, carved in stone like all the rest
of the window, 'moor' it to neighbouring windows. A sea-captain's
bust supports the roots of a cork oak, out of which climb two
elaborate masts. Seaweed, cork, anchor chains, and cables are
included elsewhere in the design, and the whole thing is topped
by the cross of the Order of Christ.

Though the Convent of Christ overshadows everything else in
Tomar, the town contains also an interesting 15th-century syna-
gogue, a lovely little Renaissance church (Nossa Senhora da
Conceicão), and other charming old buildings.

Tomar's accommodation includes a four-star hotel, a comfortable
estalagem and a good campsite.

Torralta See Portimão.

Torres Vedras

Torres Vedras is a lively small town about 70 km north of Lisbon
on the road to Obidos, Alcobaça, and Batalha. Today mainly a
commercial centre, it was the key point at the northern end of the
fortifications constructed by Wellington in 1810. Stretching all the
way to Vila Franca de Xira, the 'Lines of Torres Vedras' secured
all the land to the south between the Tagus and the sea, and
played a vital part in the eventual French withdrawal. An obelisk
erected by the town council in 1964 in a delightful small garden in
the main square commemorates Portuguese-British cooperation
and the 150th anniversary of the joint victory. The restaurant, O
Barrete Preto in Rua Paiva da Andrada, can be recommended for
its excellent Portuguese cooking and good service at reasonable
prices.

Vale de Lobo See Quarteira.

Viana do Castelo

Stretched along the River Lima's northern bank just before it joins
the sea about 70 km north of Oporto lies Viana do Castelo, a
lovely old town as well as a busy modern industrial centre, fishing
port, and holiday resort. A magnificent sandy beach runs northward along the coast west of the town.

In early medieval days Viana was just another little fishing village.
After the great voyages of discovery, however, it became
enormously prosperous, not only because of the Newfoundland
fisheries but also through its trade with the Hanseatic cities of
northern Europe. After a period of decline in the 19th century it is
again prospering, thanks to deep-sea fishing, and to its metal-
works, ceramics, and boat-building. It is famous also for its
handicrafts, and for the outstandingly picturesque Romaria of
Our Lady of the Agony (Nossa Senhora da Agonia), held every
year in the 3rd week of August and lasting 3 days, the centre point
of which is the charming little baroque chapel of the same name.
Celebrations include folk-dancing, bullfights, concerts, a cattle fair,
and an evening festival of boats and music on the river.

The old town centre, roughly rectangular in shape, contains very
attractive narrow streets lined with old houses dating largely from
the days of the town's great prosperity. In the Praça da Republica,
the former town hall, now the Turismo office, has retained its
elaborate 16th-century façade. It looks out onto a fountain of the
same date. The Misericord church (1714) with its striking azulejos,
and hospice (1589) on the old town hall's northern side are both
elegant buildings. The Parish Church south of the town hall is
mainly 14th and 15th-century, though the towers are older.

Monastery of Santa Luzia, overlooking the River Lima

Another excellent collection of 18th-century azulejos can be seen in the Municipal Museum (Museu da Cidade) in Rua Manuel Esprequeira. Pleasant public gardens slope down to the river on the town-hall side. The beach area lies to the west.

Viana is a first-rate base from which to combine enjoyment of the beach with car excursions into the lovely Minho province.

Vila do Conde

Shuttle lace has made the quiet coast resort of Vila do Conde well-known in Portugal, though it has also a few small industries. Facilities include a casino. The town lies 12 km north of Oporto, adjacent to Póvoa de Varzim. Its St Clare Convent (Mosteiro de Santa Clara) includes a 14th-century church, built originally in fortress style and containing some fine tombs. The Parish Church, also fortified, dates from the 16th century and has good Plateresque reliefs. Vila do Conde is at its liveliest during the annual Lacemakers' Festival (June 21st-24th), culminating in a grand procession on the night of St John the Baptist's Day (June 24th).

Vila Franca de Xira

An industrial town noted also for its bullfights, bulls, and traditional festivals, Vila Franca lies on the Tagus's western bank at the end of a 30-km motorway running north from Lisbon. During the Red Waistcoat (Colete Encarnado) festival in July, bulls run loose in the streets, as at Pamplona in Spain, and there are colourful processions, bullfights, music, and open-air picnics.

Vilamoura See Quarteira.

Vila Real

Vila Real is a sizeable provincial centre in Trás-os-Montes on the picturesque N2 road running north into Spain. It contains a large number of 16th to 18th-century patrician houses and is noted for the black pottery made in the region. Large quantities are brought into the town for sale at St Peter's Fair on June 29th. Vila Real boasts also a motor racing track and is a good centre from which to explore both Trás-os-Montes (see p. 34) and the Douro valley.

The Mateus estate, where the famous Mateus rosé is produced, lies about 4 km south-west. It includes a stately 18th-century residence and a garden with a lake, as well as the vineyards. There is an admission charge.

Vila Real de Santo António

Vila Real de Santo António stands on the broad Guadiana's western bank about 3 km from the sea, facing the Spanish town of Ayamonte across the river. It was built in 1774 by the Marquis of Pombal, and laid out by him in the same style as the Baixa and other parts of Lisbon. The town's purpose was to counterbalance both Ayamonte and the over-independent fishing community at nearby Monte Gordo. Today Vila Real is one of the Algarve's largest fishing and commercial centres. Its fine straight streets and elegant houses are very attractive, and it is within easy reach of the vast beach and holiday facilities at Monte Gordo.

Vila Viçosa

Vila Viçosa, 18 km from Estremoz and 35 from Elvas, is a quiet little town which today lives by its handicrafts and its history. From the 15th century until 1910 it was the chief seat of the Dukes of Bragança, whose magnificent palace is the town's chief attraction—an enormous building containing much attractive 16th, 17th, and 18th-century architecture. The old town's ramparts and castle are also worth seeing. A vast 2000-hectare (5000-acre) park, immediately north of the town, was formerly the Duke's hunting ground.

Viseu

Viseu's modern importance comes from the fact that it is the chief centre of the Dao wine-producing area. It is a sizeable provincial administrative town noted also for its handicrafts (especially lace, carpets, and black pottery). It lies 110 km south of Vila Real on the N2 leading to Coimbra and Lisbon. The old town centre is a typical tangle of narrow medieval streets, containing also a number of fine houses rather later in date. Part of the original fortifications still exist, including the stately Porta do Soar. The Cathedral (mostly 16th to 18th-century) with its 16th-century cloisters, the Cathedral Square, and the Baroque Misericord Church are among the town's notable buildings. In the 16th century Viseu rivalled Lisbon as a centre of painting, and works of that period, together with much other material of interest to art-lovers, can be seen in the Grão Vasco Museum, housed in an elegant 16th to 18th-century mansion. Viseu is quite well provided with hotels.

More Fortresses and Fortified Towns

Almourol Castle A romantic-looking fortress on a tiny island in the River Tagus, about 75 miles from Lisbon.

Castel Branco Now the capital of Beira Baixa province but formerly a fortress town guarding the frontier with Spain. Although most of its ancient monuments have been destroyed, the town is still interesting, and the gardens of the former Bishop's Palace particularly beautiful.

Castelo de Vide Close to the Spanish frontier on the main road (N118) from Santarem, it has retained its 12th-century castle and ancient Jewish quarter.

Evoramonte A tiny town between Evora and Estremoz, dominated by the castle—Roman, Moorish, and medieval—on the top of the hill.

Marvão A lovely medieval town near the Spanish border, on the Santarém road; 22 km from Portalegre and 8 km from Castelo de Vide on Route N118.

Life Portuguese Style

The People

The Portuguese are strongly Catholic, extremely conservative in their habits and outlook, but delightfully hospitable to friendly strangers. Strongly rooted in their own localities, they remain almost fiercely loyal to local traditions and celebrate local festivals with an enthusiasm that has not waned over the centuries. Despite the publicity efforts of the official tourist organisations, these religious processions and fairs have not become, by any means, mere tourist shows. In fact, you will find relatively few foreigners present at most of them. Portugal, however, is not a country that has been left behind in the past. It is thoroughly modern and, at the same time, a place where a traditional way of life still lasts.

The people are gentle, tough, quiet, friendly, and hardworking, with a passion for cleanliness—and for gardens: qualities sympathetic to the British, which could partly account for the link between the two countries. The Portuguese are England's oldest allies. The first treaty between them was signed in 1373, and with renewals and additions, it has been in force ever since. The commercial treaty of 1703, whereby British woollens were to be exchanged for port wine (see p. 31), was the effective start of even closer contact between the two countries, soon to be reinforced by the fact that they were loyal allies against Napoleon's troops in the Peninsular Wars. Though Portugal, as a matter of deliberate policy, has made no attempt as yet to keep up with other countries in the package holiday explosion of the last two decades, the British have always been among Portugal's most numerous and most welcome visitors. There are many British families who are as much at home in Portugal as in Britain, and lots of Portuguese who regard Britain and British traditions as part of their own heritage.

In the realm of art there is a wealth of lovely and often unusual items produced by Portugal's artists—outstanding amongst them the painters Cristóvão de Figueiredo, Garcia Fernandes, and Gregório Lopes; and the sculptors Nicolas Chanterene and Houdant. But despite this, many people will feel that the country's art really belongs to the thousands of unnamed craftsmen who still produce the great variety of magnificent ceramics to be found in many regions, the fine lace and handwoven rugs, carpets, bedspreads and blankets, gold and silver filigree work, superbly carved woodwork, and simple—or not so simple—baskets.

Portugal is a country where the annual fairs and even the weekly markets are a joy to attend because of the beauty and variety and reasonable price of the goods on sale. Even the decorations that ordinary fishermen paint on their boats are something decidedly out of the ordinary—as every visitor soon discovers.

Music, like art, belongs in Portugal as much to the people as to specialist composers and performers. Radio and television have made inroads, but in every province the old traditional dances are still performed to the same music and with the same songs as in centuries past. In the Algarve it is the lively *corridinho*, in Alentejo mournful *saias* and *balhas*, in Ribatejo stately *fandangos* and *escovinhos*, in Minho and Douro rhythmic and energetic *viras* and *gotas*, and so on throughout the country. Displays of folk-dance and music are organised now in tourist centres. In addition, many places have festivals of ordinary orchestral and other music.

Though commonly regarded abroad as a national tradition, the *fado* really belongs only to Lisbon and to Coimbra. It is a rather mournful song, often sung by a woman, about fate or some similarly serious topic. Accompanied by twelve-stringed Portuguese guitars with a six-stringed Spanish guitar as background, it is sung in special restaurants in Lisbon by professional *fadistas*, and in Coimbra by students. No one knows the fado's origin. It appears to have emerged in Portugal towards the end of the 18th century, possibly influenced by sailors' songs. But it is always taken very seriously—by audiences as well as performers. If you visit one of the Lisbon fado restaurants do not treat it as you might other mealtime music, and chatter happily through it: you will be thoroughly unwelcome if you do. Fado singing starts late and may last till dawn; do not arrive before 23.00. There are also a lot of amateur fado clubs.

Traditional Festivals

Portugal's traditional local festivals are very numerous and occur throughout the year. They can be divided into two main categories —*feiras*, or fairs, originally probably connected with seasonal tasks in agriculture or other occupations; and *romarias* (the word means literally 'journeys to Rome'), which are more directly religious in origin and usually include religious processions and pilgrimages to sacred shrines. These are always colourful, with brightly coloured traditional clothes, statues of saints, candles, and often musicians, including a *gaitero* or bagpiper (the instrument is less powerful than the Scottish pipes) and a tambourine player. Fireworks may be let off when the procession reaches the shrine. Each locality has its own traditions.

Once the religious celebration is completed, secular festivities begin. Folk-dancing, fireworks, music, stalls selling local handi-crafts, and sometimes a sort of gigantic mass picnic are the form the festivities usually take. Many *feiras* and *romarias* last more than one day. Perhaps their most attractive feature is the fact that they are still very much a product of local life, intended for the local people's edification and entertainment. Only those at Viana do Castelo and Fátima have achieved much international fame, and even here you will find relatively few foreign visitors. A list of the more important and more colourful *feiras* and *romarias* is given on pp. 20-21.

Oxen from the Minho, with intricately carved wooden yokes (p. 51)

Bullfighting may form part of the celebrations at certain fairs. But it is really a separate traditional sport, practised from Easter to October. The Portuguese version has developed very differently from Spain's. Since the 18th century it has been forbidden to kill a bull in the ring: the object is to master and immobilise it.

The bullfight (*tourada*) opens with a spectacular procession of all the participants. Then the horsemen (*cavaleiros*) provoke the bull by their riding, and at the same time wear it down with darts (*farpas*, the equivalent of the Spanish *banderillas*) stuck into fleshy muscles. At a suitable moment the final stage (*pega*) begins. The horsemen give way to eight *moços de forcado* on foot. Their leader's job is, first, to demonstrate his skill by jumping over the bull's horns, then to seize the animal by the horns while the others help immobilise it. If this proves impossible, he has to seize its withers from the side while the others pull on the animal's tail and so prevent it from moving. The bull is usually slaughtered in the normal way the following day.

The best fighting bulls are bred in the Ribatejo province, and the best bullfights take place in Lisbon, Santarém, and Vila Franca de Xira.

Sport

Portugal is much better provided with sports facilities than most people realise. Espinho and Estoril, for instance, have had 18-hole golf courses of good quality for many years. Newer and even more lavish 18-hole courses have been built in more recent years near Caparica, and at Penina (designed and managed by Henry Cotton), Vale de Lobo, Quinta do Lago and Vilamoura on the Algarve coast. Additional 9-hole courses exist at Praia de Granja (near Espinho), Vidago (inland north-east), and Praia de Porto Novo (south of Peniche). Also at Vale de Lobo and Penina—where a further 9 holes under construction will complete a second 18-hole course.

Two 18-hole courses are being built at Monte Gordo. Tennis courts too, are available in most sizeable towns and resorts.

Deep-sea angling, spear fishing, and scuba diving are of an equally high standard. Virtually every sizeable coast resort can provide facilities for sea fishing, though the types of catch vary. From the extreme north to the Tagus estuary, bass, grey bream, grey and red mullet, eels, sole, and pout whiting are the main fish caught. From Sesimbra southwards and all along the Algarve coast big-game and deep-sea catches include swordfish, tunny, and various types of shark. Troll-fishing produces bass, coalfish, bluefish, bream, and other varieties. Tope, bonito, mullet, conger and moray eels, and much else can be caught inshore. The Hotel Espadarte at Sesimbra, and the Batador restaurant at Sagres (near the Hotel de Baleeira) cater specially for deep-sea anglers, though boats and equipment can be hired at most larger resorts.

Neither sea fishing nor spear fishing requires a permit. Both can be practised throughout the year. Areas specially recommended for spear fishing are: Peniche, Berlenga Island, Sesimbra, Sines, and— best of all—Sagres. Visibility off Sesimbra can be poor in winter, and off Peniche occasional cloudiness occurs. Conditions otherwise are normally good. Underwater life is particularly rich and plentiful at the Algarve coast's western end.

Scuba diving is similarly free of restrictions, though you should ask locally about areas that may be forbidden for security or other reasons. Clear waters, rocky headlands and coves, and the tremendous variety of marine life make it very attractive. Aqualung clubs exist in many towns and resorts. Air-bottles can be refilled in Lisbon, Oporto, and the Algarve.

Sailing and water-skiing are as yet relatively little developed. Only the biggest resorts, such as Cascais, Albufeira, Faro, and Praia da Rocha, have well-established arrangements for water-skiing; one obvious reason is the fact that the Atlantic which washes Portugal's shores is not the smoothest of oceans. And while every sizeable harbour can find moorings for visiting yachts, Portugal's first modern-style yacht marina has only recently been built at Vilamoura on the Algarve coast. Further developments will certainly be on the way.

Portugal's lakes and rivers throughout the country offer good fishing for trout, barbel, carp, club and other species—also salmon in some areas. Sea trout and brown trout can be caught in northern rivers such as the Minho and Lima. Permits are not required on Sundays or public holidays, nor by foreign visitors. If you do buy one (from the local town hall), the cost is negligible. Fishing is, however, legally forbidden during the hours of darkness, and there are closed seasons for salmon and trout (August 1st to end of February) and for all other species (March 15th-July 31st).

Riding is very popular, particularly in resorts and holiday areas, and there is no shortage of horses for hire. Centres have been developed mainly in the newer resorts and the bigger towns such as Leiria, Oporto, and of course Lisbon. But they are spreading to smaller places too.

Among less widely practised sports a certain amount of mainly rough shooting is possible. An import permit for shotguns and up to 400 cartridges must be obtained from the Customs on arrival, and a game licence obtained after payment of a 1000$ deposit against the guns' re-export. Winter skiing is possible in the Serra da Estrela. Roller skating is surprisingly popular among the Portuguese. Rinks can be found in most sizeable towns.

Entertainment

For evening entertainment Portugal can provide standard-type discothèques, mainly in the Cascais-Estoril region and in the chief international resorts. In these and other places, especially Lisbon, you will also find what are called *boîtes* and *nightclubs*. Boîte is, of course, the French word for nightclub. In Portuguese, however, it often indicates what in France is known—with the aid of an equally misused English word—as *un dancing*—a bar where you can dance. The term nightclub is applied mostly to places where you can dine and enjoy a floorshow as well as dance. Distinctions between the different types of nightspot are, however, becoming blurred. Some discothèques and boîtes also serve dinner.

In Estoril the smartest nightclub is in the Casino, which also offers gambling. Other casinos exist at Espinho, Figueira da Foz, Cascais, Póvoa de Varzim, and Vila do Conde. The Algarve's first Casino opened at Penina in 1973, followed by another at Vilamoura, and a third at Monte Gordo, all under the same management. All have nightclubs, bars, and restaurants as well as gambling. Visitors are legally obliged to show passports when entering a casino.

Apart from the 'fado restaurants' in Lisbon (p. 71), there are plenty of bars in every corner of the country where men can, and do, go to enjoy themselves. Respectable females, however, do not go into most bars, not even with their menfolk, unless they are foreign visitors inside an international tourist precinct. Women's special preserve, in Lisbon and other big towns, is the *tearooms* where they gather for a 'five o'clock', tea (or coffee) and cream cakes.

Most towns and resorts have cinemas, open seven days a week, where mostly British and American films are run in English with Portuguese sub-titles. Lisbon, Oporto, and quite a number of other towns have theatres. In addition, there are the folklore displays and the concerts, given during music festivals in the larger centres, already mentioned (p. 71).

Bullfighting apart, soccer is easily the most popular spectator sport, with grounds in most large towns. Vila Real has a well-established motor-racing circuit and another opened recently at Estoril.

Food

Portuguese cooking is best described by the French term *paysan*, in the real meaning of 'belonging to the country'. The ingredients are fresh, not imported or frozen. They appear on the table when they are in season. They are plentiful and tasty, and the dishes made with them are filling. The richness extends to the sauces and seasonings, usually extremely spicy. Yet at the same time there is little that is likely to upset stomachs accustomed to less exuberant delights.

Soups are varied and unusual. *Caldo verde*, strictly belonging to the Minho province and made with mashed potatoes and finely chopped cabbage, has become a sort of national dish. Small slices of *tora*, a sort of black pudding, are added during cooking. But there are lots of other soups, including the *açordas*, made with bread. The Alentejo province's *sopa de coentros*, for example, floats a poached egg on a base of coriander, garlic, olive oil and bread, and is delicious. In the south a *gaspacho*, usually made with tomatoes, onions, cucumbers, pimentos, garlic, and vinegar, is served cold. Fish and shellfish soup (*sopa de peixe* and *sopa de mariscos*) is very popular. The term *caldeirada* is applied to both fish soup and fish stew. A *caldeirada a fragateira* resembles a southern French bouillabaisse, with a great mixture of ingredients. Among fish dishes *bacalhau á gomes de sá* (stewed cod with, among other things, potatoes, eggs, and olives) is regarded as something of a national dish. But you will get fish and shellfish of every sort served in a large number of different ways. Fresh sardines are grilled over charcoal and served with potatoes and green peppers (*sardinhas assadas*). Lampreys (*lampreias*) and eels (*enguias*) are popular in the north. Crayfish (*lagostas*) may be served jugged, and giant prawns (*gambas*) baked. In the Algarve, oysters are cooked in a copper vessel with aromatic herbs and sausages.

Apart from pork (*porco*) and roast kid (*cabrito*), Portuguese meat is not in itself outstanding. But you will get many tasty casseroles and pot roasts. Pork is often smoked and served as cutlets (*paios*) or ham (*presunto*); sometimes smoked pig's tongue (*linguíça*), is eaten, or the pork mixed with oysters or mussels (*porco á Alentejana*). It is also added to other dishes, such as the *cozido á Portuguesa*, a beef hotpot with potatoes, vegetables, and rice. Other delicacies include tripe and roast sucking pig (*leitão assado*).

Vegetables are plentiful and varied in season. Spinach and asparagus are particularly good. Tomatoes are used in great quantity, especially in the excellent salads. Rice appears in innumerable guises, as both vegetable and dessert—it is in fact grown in parts of Portugal.

Among cheeses those made from ewes' milk, such as *queija de Castelo Branco* and *queija de Azeitão*, make specially good eating between May and October. The goats' milk cheeses—*cabreiro, robaçal,* and others—are also exceptionally tasty. If you are offered a local cheese, try it. More often than not you will get a very pleasant surprise.

Fruit is abundant, varied, and good as the vegetables. It includes raspberries, plums, melons, oranges, strawberries, peaches, and figs. But the Portuguese love to end a meal with dessert dishes whose lavish use of sugar betrays their oriental origin. Large numbers of towns and regions take pride in local dessert and pastry specialities. Torres Vedras's delicious *pasteis de feijão* are just one example—and not a well-known one either. Elsewhere you may be offered such things as *ovos moles*, a confection of egg yolks and sugar prepared in a shell-shaped mould.

Many other dishes also use eggs. The most popular way of serving rice, for instance, is known as *arroz doce*. The rice is first cooked with vanilla, lemon peel, and sugar. Then the vanilla pod and lemon peel are removed and egg yolks beaten in. The dish is served cold, sprinkled with cinnamon. Figs and almonds prevail, however, in Algarve desserts.

I must add one word of warning. Portuguese recipes have never been standardised to the extent that most French dishes have. Every cook has his (or her) own ideas, so that Portuguese cooking retains many of the delights—or drawbacks— of what French gastronomic writers call *cuisine impromptue*.

Drink

Portugal produces a considerable variety of table wines, many of which are not exported outside the producing region. If in doubt you can always ask for a *vinho da região* (local wine), which may be *tinto* (red), *branco* (white), or *rosé*. A straightforward, ordinary cheap wine is called *vinho de mesa* (table wine), often served in a jug or carafe.

The products of two wine regions, however, are particularly worth sampling—apart from port and Madeira, which demand separate discussion. These are the gently sparkling light-coloured white *vinhos verdes,* of low alcoholic content, from the Minho and lower Douro valley, and the red and white wines from the Dão valley. The *Colares* (red) and *Bucelas* (white) wines are also good. Many others also deserve to be better known, such as those from Ribatejo province, from Torres Vedras, Alcobaça, Chamusca, Agueda, and Lafões, and the Pinhel rosé. Mateus rosé needs no introduction.

Till very recent years, port was regarded—in Britain at least—as virtually a British drink, even though the after-dinner port-passing ritual of great houses, service messes, and Oxbridge senior common rooms is vanishing slowly into the past. But for some reason never fathomed, British port-drinkers take only the medium or sweet red port, the dessert wine, and neglect completely the dry or very dry white port which makes an excellent aperitif, much appreciated in Portugal and elsewhere.

Madeira comes from the island which has been a Portuguese possession for over 550 years. But what we call Madeira is usually the dessert wine known to the Portuguese as Boal. Like port, it has also a dry, amber-coloured aperitif version, named Sercial. The most famous dessert version, Malmsey, deep red and honey-flavoured, is today difficult to find.

A number of brandies, liqueurs, and what the French call *alcools* (similar to *framboise* and other drinks from eastern France) are produced in Portugal, often on a strictly local basis. They are worth sampling. Some are very acceptable.

When you are not drinking wine you will find that Portugal bottles good spa waters. Luso is non-fizzy. Vidago, Pedras Salgadas, Vimeiro and others—all from known spas—are fizzy in greater or less degree. Various types of fruit juice are available, together with soft drinks like Pepsi Cola and a local speciality, *capilé*, a sort of sarsaparilla. Beers are of the light lager type. Coffee, including the Portuguese-manufactured instant type, is usually very good. It is served strong and black—except at breakfast—unless milk (*leite*) is specifically asked for. Pasteurised milk is available only from special shops, but litre bottles of sterilised milk, with a rather different taste, can be bought everywhere.

A Pronunciation Guide

Stress

In words ending with a vowel, *m*, *n*, or *s*, the stress is on the next to last
syllable. Words ending in consonants other than the above are stressed on
the last syllable. Stresses other than these are marked with an accent.

Vowels

The vowel sound is altered according to whether it is in a stressed or
unstressed syllable.

a	as in *f*a*ther*	—in a stressed syllable, or *á*, sometimes in an unstressed syllable, too
	as in *a*bout	—in an unstressed syllable, or *â*
e	as in s*e*t	—in most stressed syllables, or *é*
	as in f*a*te	—in certain stressed syllables, or *ê*
	almost silent	—in an unstressed syllable, especially when final
i	as in mach*i*ne—	
o	as in n*o*rth	—in a stressed syllable, *ó*, or followed by *l*+consonant
	as in n*o*te	—in a stressed syllable, *ô* (the commonest sound)
	as in b*oo*t	—in an unstressed syllable
u	as in b*oo*t	—in a stressed syllable
	as in f*oo*t	—in an unstressed syllable

Consonants

The consonant is pronounced differently according to whether its position
in a word or syllable is initial, medial, or final.

b	silent when final	
c	as in *c*at	
	before *e* or *i*, or *ç*, as in *s*at	
ch	as in *sh*oe	
d	as in *d*og—initially before vowels	
	medially after *l*, *n*, *r*	
	as in *th*ough—in all other cases	
g	as in *g*ot	
	before *e* or *i* as in a*z*ure	
gu	as in *g*ot	
h	always silent	
j	as in a*z*ure	
m	silent when final or before consonants (except *b* or *p*), but nazalises the preceding vowel	
n	silent when final or before *d*, *t*, *k*, *g*, but nazalises the preceding vowel	
qu	as in *qu*een	
	before *e* or *i* as in *c*at	
r	as in ve*r*y—between vowels, medially or finally in a syllable	
r	trilled—beginning of syllable, or doubled	
s	as in *s*un—initially, after consonants, or doubled	
	as in pre*s*ent—between vowels	
	as in *sh*oe—finally, or before consonants *p*, *k*, *t*, *f*	
	as in plea*s*ure—before consonants other than the above	
x	as in *sh*oe—in most positions	
	as in *s*o—also between vowels	
	as in *z*eal—before a vowel, or in prefix *ex*-	
z	as in *z*ebra—initially, and medially	
	as in *sh*all—finally	

Vocabulary

Everyday Expressions

Mr.	*Senhor*
Mrs.	*Senhora*
Miss	*Menina*
Please	*Por favor*
Thank you	*Obrigado*
Good morning	*Bom dia*
Good day	*Bom dia*
Good afternoon	*Boa tarde*
Good evening (until sunset)	*Boa tarde*
Good night (after sunset)	*Boa noite*
Good-bye	*Adeus*
Yes	*Sim*
No	*Não*
How do you do?	*Como está?*
Very well, and you?	*Muito bem, e Você?*
Excuse me (pardon me)	*Desculpe*
Excuse me (with your permission)	*Com licença*
I am English	*Sou inglês* (a)
Do you speak English?	*Fala inglês?*
I cannot speak Portuguese	*Não falo português*
I want . . .	*Quero . . .*
Come in	*Entre*
That's all right	*Está bem*
You are most kind	*O senhor* } *é muito amável* *A senhora* }
Never mind	*Não tem importância*
Don't worry	*Não se preocupe*
Am I disturbing you?	*Estou a incomodar?*
May I introduce . . .	*Permite-me apresentar . . .*
I don't mind	*Não me importo*
I don't think so	*Não creio*
I am very grateful to you	*Estou-lhe muito agradecido*
What is this (that)?	*O que é isto (aquilo)?*
Like this (that)	*Como isto (aquilo)*
This (that) side	*Este (aquele) lado*
It is (was) wonderful	*É (foi) maravilhoso*
Will this (that) do?	*Serve isto (isso)?*
I agree	*Estou de acordo*
Help yourself	*Sirva-se*
What is the time?	*Que horas são?*

In difficulty

Can you help me?	*Pode ajudar-me?*
I am looking for . . .	*Estou à procura . . .*
Can you direct me to . . .?	*Pode dizer-me como chegar a . . .?*
I am lost	*Estou perdido*
Where is the British Consulate?	*Onde é o Consulado Britânico?*
Speak slowly	*Fale devagar*
I am hungry (thirsty)	*Tenho fome (sede)*
I am busy (tired)	*Estou ocupado (cansado)*
I am sorry	*Sinto muito. Desculpe*
What a pity!	*Que pena!*
What do you want?	*O que deseja?*
What do you mean?	*Que quer o senhor (a) dizer?*
I do not know	*Não sei*

I do not understand	*Não compreendo*
I do not agree	*Não estou de acordo*
I do not like it	*Não gosto disso*
I must go now	*Tenho que ir embora*
It is forbidden	*Prolbe-se*
It is urgent	*É urgente*
Hurry up!	*Depressa!*
Be careful!	*Cuidado!*
Look out!	*Atenção!*
Be quiet!	*Esteja calado (a)!*
Leave me alone!	*Deixe-me!*
I shall call a policeman	*Chamarei um policia*
Help!	*Socorro!*

after	*depois*	more	*mais*
against	*contra*	much	*muito*
agreed	*de acordo*	near	*perto*
all	*todo*	next	*próximo*
almost	*quase*	now	*agora*
among	*entre*	not	*não*
before	*antes que*	okay	*está bem*
behind	*atrás*	on	*sôbre*
below	*abaixo de*	outside	*por fora*
beside	*ao lado de*	over	*acima de*
between	*entre*	perhaps	*talvez*
cold	*frio*	quick	*rápido*
downstairs	*lá embaixo*	right	*direito*
elsewhere	*parte noutra*	slow	*devagar*
enough	*bastante*	somebody	*alguém*
everybody	*todos*	something	*alguma coisa*
everything	*tudo*	that	*aquilo*
everywhere	*em toda a parte*	there	*ali*
except	*excepto*	these	*estes, estas*
far	*distante*	this	*este, esta*
for	*por, para*	those	*aqueles*
here	*aquí*	through	*através*
hot	*quente*	too	*também*
in	*em*	towards	*para*
in front of	*em frente de*	until	*até*
inside	*por dentro*	upstairs	*em cima*
last	*último*	very	*muito*
left	*esquerdo*	welcome	*bem-vindo*
less	*menos*	when	*quando*
listen	*escutar*	where	*onde*
little	*pequeno*	why	*porquê*
look	*olhar*	without	*sem*
many	*muitos*		

Accommodation

I have reserved a room (two rooms)	*Reservei um (dois) quarto(s)*
I wish to stay for . . .	*Quero ficar até . . .*
I do not want meals	*Não quero refeiçoes*
I shall not be here for lunch	*Não estarei para o almoço*
May I take a packed lunch?	*Posso ter um piquenique?*
I want breakfast only	*Só quero pequeno almoço*
I want a room with one bed (two beds, a double bed)	*Quero um quarto com uma cama (duas camas, cama de casal)*

I want a room with a private
   bathroom
I am on a diet
I cannot eat . . .
What are your charges, including
   (excluding) meals?
What time is breakfast (lunch,
   dinner, tea)?
I should like something cheaper
Have you a room with a better
   view?
I want to leave early tomorrow
Wake me at . . .
Can I have my clothes pressed?
Can I have my shoes cleaned?
Can I drink the water from the tap?
I want a hot bath
Is there a plug for my electric razor?

What is the voltage?
I have some things to be washed
Will you get this mended?
When will they be ready?
When does the hotel close?
I shall be very late
May I have a key?
Is there a night porter?
Forward my mail to this address

Quero um quarto com banho
   privativo
Estou em regime de dieta
Não posso comer . . .
Quais são os preços, com (sem)
   comida?
A que horas é o pequeno almoço
   (o almoço, o jantar, o chá)?
Quero uma coisa mais baratà
Tem um quarto com melhor vista?

Quero ir-me embora amanhã cedo
Desperte-me às . . . horas
Podem passar a minha roupa?
Podem engraxar os meus sapatos?
Posso beber a água da torneira?
Quero um banho quente
Há uma tomada para a minha
   máquina de barbear?
Qual é a voltagem?
Tenho roupa para lavar
Pode mandar reparar isto?
Quando estarão prontos?
Quando fecha o hotel?
Voltarei muito tarde
Pode dar-me uma chave?
Há um porteiro de noite?
Faça o favor de remeter o meu
   correio para este endereço

armchair	a poltrona
bath	o banho
bathroom	o quarto de banho
bed	a cama
bedroom	o quarto de dormir
bedroom, single	o quarto para uma pessoa
double	o quarto para duas pessoas
with twin beds	o quarto com duas camas
with a double bed	o quarto com cama de casal
bell	a campaínha
better	melhor
bill	a conta
blanket	o cobertor
blind	a cortiña
boarding-house	a pensão
board (full)	a pensão completa
board (half)	meia-pensão
bulb (electric light)	a lâmpada
chair	a cadeira
chambermaid	a empregada de quarto

coat-hanger	o cabide
cook	o cozinheiro
curtain	a cortina
dining-room	a sala de jantar
eiderdown	o edredon
floor (storey)	o andar
hotel	o hotel
hotel-keeper	o recepcionista
hot-water bottle	a botija
key	a chave
large	grande
larger	maior
lavatory	a toilette
lift	o elevador
manager	o gerente
mattress	o colchão
office	o escritorio
pillow	a almofada
plug (electric)	a tomada
porter	o porteiro
proprietor	o proprietário
quiet	sossegado
quieter	mais sossegado
radiator	o radiador
reading-lamp	o candeeiro
sheet	o lençol
shower	o chuveiro

shutter	*o postigo*
sitting-room	*a sala de extar*
small	*pequeno*
smaller	*mais pequeno*
soap	*o sabonete*
staircase	*as escadas*
switch (light)	*o interruptor da luz*

table	*a mesa*
tap	*a torneira*
terrace	*o terraço*
towel	*a toalha*
wardrobe	*o guarda-roupa*
washbasin	*o lavatório*
window	*a janela*

Beach and Bathing

Where is the beach?	*Onde é a praia?*
Where can I bathe?	*Onde posso banhar-me?*
Is it safe to swim here?	*Posso banhar-me aquí sem perigo?*
Is it deep or shallow?	*É funda ou não a água?*
Is the beach sandy or pebbly?	*A praia é arenosa ou pedregosa?*
I want to hire a . . .	*Quero alugar um . . .*
Where can I change?	*Onde posso mudar-me?*
I cannot swim very well	*Não sei nadar muito bem*
Help! Someone is drowning!	*Socorro! Afoga-se alguém!*
Can I go underwater swimming here?	*Posso nadar debaixo de água aquí?*
Bathing prohibited	*E proíbido tomar banho*

air mattress	*a colchão pneumática*
bathe	*o banho*
bathing cap	*a touca de banho*
bathing costume	*o fato de banho*
bathing hat	*a touca de banho*
beach	*a praia*
beach umbrella	*o guarda-sol*
boat	*o barco*
buoy	*a bóia*
canoe	*a canoa*
cliff	*o penhasco*
coast	*a costa*
crab	*o caranguejo*
current	*a corrente*
danger	*o perigo*
deckchair	*a cadeira de lona*
dive, to	*mergulhar*
fish, to	*pescar*
flippers	*as nadadeiras*
harpoon	*o arpão*
jelly-fish	*a alforreca*
knife	*a faca*

lifebelt	*o cinto de salvação*
lighthouse	*o farol*
mask	*a máscara*
octopus	*o polvo*
pebble	*o calhau*
raft	*a jangada*
rock	*a rocha*
rowing-boat	*o barco a remos*
sand	*a areia*
sea	*o mar*
shark	*o tubarão*
shell	*a concha*
snorkel tube	*o tubo para respiração*
speargun	*a espingarda de arpão*
sun	*o sol*
sunshade	*o toldo*
surf board	*a tábua de surf*
tide	*a maré*
towel	*a toalha*

Camping

Where does this road lead?	*Onde vai dar este caminho?*
How far is it to . . .?	*A que distância fica . . .?*
What is the name of this place?	*Como é que se chama este lugar?*
Is there a Youth Hostel near here?	*Há um albergue da juventude perto?*
Can we cut across country?	*Podemos atravessar o campo?*
We are lost	*Perdemos o caminho*
We are looking for a camping site	*Estamos à procura dum parque de campismo*
May we light a fire?	*Podemos fazer uma fogueira?*
Where is the toilet (washroom)?	*Onde é a toilette (lavatorio)?*

I should like to hire a bicycle — *Quero alugar uma bicicleta*
Where can I buy methylated spirit (paraffin)? — *Onde posso comprar alcóol desnaturado (parafina)?*

bottle opener	*o saca-rolhas*
bucket	*o balde*
camp	*acampamento*
camping equipment	*o equipamento de campismo*
camping site	*o parque de campismo*
candle	*a vela*
caravan	*a roulotte*
country	*o campo*
field	*o prado*
ground sheet	*o lençol impermeável*
haversack	*o farnel*
hitch-hike	*pedir boleia*
hill	*a colina*
inn	*a estalagem*
lake	*o lago*
matches	*os fósforos*
mountain	*a montanha*
path	*o caminho*
penknife	*o canivete*
picnic	*o piquenique*
river	*o rio*
road	*a estrada*
rope	*a corda*
rubbish	*o lixo*
sandwich	*a sanduíche*
saucepan	*a panela*
sleeping-bag	*o saco de dormir*
store	*a loja*
tent	*a barraca*
tent peg	*a estaca para barraca*
thermos	*o termos*
tin opener	*o abre latas*
torch	*a pilha*
waterproof	*o impermeável*
wood	*a lenha*

Church

Where is a Roman Catholic church (Protestant church, synagogue, mosque)? — *Onde há uma igreja católica (igreja protestante, sinagoga, mesquita)?*
At what time are the services held? — *A que horas têm oficios religiosos?*
Is there an English-speaking priest? — *Há um padre que fale inglês?*

Colours

black	*preto*
blue	*azul*
brown	*castanho*
cream	*creme*
crimson	*carmesim*
fawn	*beige*
gold	*dourado*
green	*verde*
grey	*cinzento*
orange	*côr de laranja*
pink	*côr-de-rosa*
purple	*purpura*
red	*vermelho*
scarlet	*escarlate*
silver	*prateado*
violet	*violeta*
white	*branco*
yellow	*amarelo*

Days of the Week

Sunday	*domingo*
Monday	*segunda-feira*
Tuesday	*terça-feira*
Wednesday	*quarta-feira*
Thursday	*quinta-feira*
Friday	*sexta-feira*
Saturday	*sábado*

Months

January	*Janeiro*
February	*Fevereiro*
March	*Março*
April	*Abril*
May	*Maio*
June	*Junho*
July	*Julho*
August	*Agosto*
September	*Setembro*
October	*Outubro*
November	*Novembro*
December	*Dezembro*

Entertainment

Where is a good (cheap) night club? — *Onde há uma boîte boa (barata)?*

Would you care to dance? — Gostaria de dançar?
Where can I dance? — Onde posso dançar?
What would you like to drink? — O que quer beber?

band	a banda	dance hall	a sala de baile
box	o camarote	entertainments	as diversões
box office	a bilheteira	film	o filme
casino	o casino	gaming-room	a sala de jogo
cinema	o cinema	interval	o intervalo
cloakroom ticket	a senha do vestiário	night club	a boîte
concert hall	a sala de concêrto	seat	o lugar
dance	a baile	stage	o palco
dance, to	dançar	stall	a plateia
		theatre	o teatro

Food and Restaurants

Where is a good (cheap) restaurant? — Onde há um restaurante bom (barato)?
Where is a quick-service restaurant? — Onde há um restaurante de serviço rápido?
Where is a good restaurant for seafood? — Onde há um bom restaurante para mariscos?
Where is a good restaurant for dishes? — Onde há um bom restaurante para pratos locais?
Can we lunch here? — Podemos almoçar aquí?
I should like a table near the window — Quero uma mesa perta da janela
I only want a snack — Só quero uma refeição leve
I am in a hurry — Estou com pressa
I should like to wash my hands — Quero lavar as mãos
Have you the menu? — Tem o menú?
I like it underdone (medium) (well done) — Quero-o mal passado (meio passado) (bem passado)
A little more — Um pouco mais
That's too much — Isso é demais
I did not order this — Não pedi isto
Bring me another — Traga-me outro
This is cold — Isto está frio
I have had enough — Já tive o suficiente
May I have the bill? — Traz-me a conta?
Is the service included? — Está incluido o servíco?
Is this correct? — Está correcto?
Please check it — Faça o favor de verificá-lo
I made a mistake — Enganei-me
I'm sorry — Desculpe
Keep the change — Fique com o troco
We enjoyed the meal — Gostámos muito da refeição

ashtray	o cinzeiro	glass	o copo
bar	o bar	knife	a faca
bill	a conta	meal	a refeição
bottle	a garrafa	menu, bill of fare	o menú
canned	enlatado		
clean	limpo	not clean	não está limpo
cork	a rolha	not fresh	não está fresco
cup	a chávena	plate	o prato
dirty	sujo	saucer	o pires
fork	o garfo	serviette, napkin	o guardanapo
fresh	fresco	spoon	o colher

tablecloth	a toalha de mesa
teapot	o bule de chá
tip	a gorjeta
waiter	o empregado de mesa
waiter (head)	o chefe de mesa
waiter (wine)	o empregado de mesa
waitress	a empregada de mesa
water-jug	o jarro
wine list	a lista de vinhos
food	
apple	a maçã
apricot	o damasco
artichoke	a alcachofra
asparagus	o espargo
bacon	o toucinho
banana	a banana
beans	o feijão
beef	a carne de vaca
biscuit	a bolacha
bread (white)	o pão
bread (brown)	o pão de centeio
butter	a manteiga
cabbage	a couve
cake	o bolo
carrot	a cenoura
cauliflower	a couve-flor
caviare	o caviar
celery	o aipo
cheese	o queijo
cherries	as cerejas
chicken	o frango
chocolate	o chocolate
chops	as costeletas
crab	o caranguejo
crayfish	o caranguejo de rio
cream	a nata
cucumber	o pepino
dessert	a sobremesa
egg	o ovo
figs	os figos
fish	o peixe
fruit	a fruta
game	a caça
garlic	o alho
grapes	as uvas
grapefruit	a toranja
ham	o fiambre
honey	o mel
hors-d'oeuvres	os hors-d'oeuvres
ice	o gelo
ice-cream	o gelado
jam	a compota
kidney	o rim
lamb	o cordeiro
lemon	o limão
lettuce	a alface
liver	o fígado
lobster	a lagosta
marmalade	o doce de laranja
melon	o melão
mushroom	o cogumelo
mussels	os mexilhões
mustard	a mostarda
mutton	o carneiro
oil	o azeite
olive oil	o azeite
onion	a cebola
orange	a laranja
oyster	a ostra
pastry	a pastelaria
peach	o pêssego
peanuts	os amendoins
pear	a pera
peas	as ervilhas
pepper	a pimenta
pickles	os pickles
pineapple	o ananás
plum	a ameixa
pork	o porco
potato	a batata
prawn	o camarão
prunes	as ameixas secas
raisins	as passas
raspberry	a framboesa
rice	o arroz
roll	o pãozinho
salad	a salada
salmon	o salmão
salt	o sal
sardine	a sardinha
sauce	o molho
sausage (beef)	o salami
sausage (pork)	a salsicha
scampi	os camarões
seafood	os mariscos
shrimp	o camarão
snail	o caracol
sole	o linguado
soup (clear)	o caldo
soup (thick)	a sopa
spinach	o espinafre
steak	o bife
strawberry	o morango
sugar	o açúcar
toast	a torrada
tomato	o tomate
trout	a truta
vanilla	a baunilha
veal	a vitela
vegetables	os legumes
vinegar	o vinagre

Drink

What would you like to drink?		O que gostaria de beber?	
What do you suggest?		O que sugere?	
I should like . . .		Eu queria . . .	
Your health!		À sua saude!	

alcoholic drink	a bebida alcoólica	mineral water	a água mineral
apéritif	o aperitivo	mug	a caneca
beer (light)	a cerveja	nip	o trago
beer (dark)	a cerveja (preta)	non-alcoholic	sem álcool
bottle (half)	(meia) garrafa	orangeade	a laranjada
brandy	a aguardente	port	o vinho do Porto
carafe	o jarro	rum	o rum
champagne	a champanha	sherry	o xerez
chocolate	o chocolate	soda water	a soda
cider	a cidra	tea (with milk)	o chá (com leite)
cocktail	o cocktail	tea (with lemon)	o chá (de limão)
coffee (white)	o café com leite	tea (without milk)	o chá (sem leite)
coffee (black)	o café		
gin	o gin	tonic water	a água tónica
glass	o copo	vermouth	o vermute
ice	o gelo	vodka	a vodka
jug	o jarro	water	a água
lager	a cerveja dinamarquesa	whisky	o uisque
		wine, dry	o vinho seco
lemon	o limão	sweet	o vinho doce
lemonade	a limonada	red	o vinho tinto
liqueur	o licor	rosé	o vinho rosado
milk	o leite	white	o vinho branco
milk shake	o batido	local	o vinho da casa

Health

Send for a doctor	Chame um médico
It is broken	Está quebrado
Have you any bandages?	Tem ligaduras?
Do not move him (her)	Não o (a) mova
I am not feeling well	Não-me sinto bem
I have a pain here	Tenho um dôr aqui
I have a headache	Tenho uma dôr de cabeça
I have a sore throat	Tenho a garganta dorida
My stomach is upset	Tenho o estômago indispôsto
I feel much better	Sinto-me muito melhor
Can you recommend a dentist?	Pode recomendar um dentista?
I have a toothache	Doem-me os dentes
I want it out	Tire-mo
I should like an injection	Quero uma injeção
You are hurting me	Doi-me
Can you make up this prescription?	Pode preparar-me esta receita?
When will it be ready?	Quando estará pronto?
Can you give me a remedy for . . .?	Pode dar-me um remédio para . . .?
For external use only	Só para emprego exterior
One teaspoonful (tablespoonful) in a glass of water	Uma colher de chá (de sopa) num copo de água

accident	o acidente	bite	a picada
ambulance	a ambulância	bleeding	o sangrar
bandage	a ligadura	blister	a bolha

boil	*o furúnculo*		sprain	*a entorce*
burn (scald)	*a queimadura (escaldadura)*		sting	*a picada*
			stomach-ache	*a dor de estómago*
cold	*a constipação*		sunburn	*a queimadura de sol*
constipation	*a prisão de ventre*			
cough	*a tosse*		sunstroke	*a insolação*
cramp	*a cãibra*		surgery	*a sala de médico*
cut	*o corte*		swelling	*o inchaço*
dangerous	*perigoso*		temperature	*a temperatura*
dentist	*o dentista*		toothache	*a dor de dentes*
diarrhoea	*a diarreia*		vomit	*o vómito*
diet	*a dieta*		wound	*a ferida*

chemist

doctor	*o médico*		aspirin	*a aspirina*
faint	*o desmaio*		contraceptive	*o preservativo*
fever	*o febre*		cotton-wool	*o algodão em rama*
filling (stopping)	*a obturação*			
gas	*o gás*		gargle	*o gargarejo*
hay-fever	*o febre do feno*		gauze	*o gaze*
headache	*a dor de cabeça*		iodine	*o iôdo*
hospital	*o hospital*		laxative	*o laxante*
illness	*a doença*		medicine	*a medicina*
indigestion	*a indigestão*		powder (talcum)	*o talco*
injection	*a injecção*		prescription	*a receita*
insomnia	*a insónia*		quinine	*o quinino*
nausea	*as náuseas*		sanitary towel	*o pano higiênico*
nurse	*a enfermeira*		sleeping-pill	*a pilula para fazer dormir*
pain	*a dor*			
poison	*o veneno*		smelling-salts	*os sais*
remedy	*o remédio*		sticking-plaster	*o penso adesivo*
sick, to feel	*ter náuseas, enjoado*		toilet paper	*o papel higiênico*
			vaseline	*a vaselina*
sore throat	*a garganta dorida*			

Money/Banks

Where is the nearest bank?	*Onde é o Banco mais próximo?*
May I see the manager?	*Posso falar com o Gerente?*
Will you cash this (travellers') cheque?	*Faça o favor de trocar este cheque (de viagem)?*
What is the exchange rate for the pound sterling?	*Qual é taxa de câmbio da libra esterlina?*
How much is this worth?	*Quanto vale isto?*
I should like some small change	*Quero algumas moedas*

cash, to	*receber na caixa*		money exchange bureau	*o cambista*
change	*o troco*			
cheque	*o cheque*		note	*a nota*
coin	*a moeda*		pound sterling	*a libra esterlina*
exchange	*o câmbio*		rate	*a taxa*
letter of credit	*a carta de crédito*		travellers' cheque	*o cheque de viagem*
money	*o dinheiro*			

Motoring

Do you know the road to . . .?	*Conhece o caminho para . . .?*
How far is it to . . .?	*A que distancia . . .?*
I want some petrol (oil, water)	*Quero gasolina (óleo, água)*
I need . . . litres	*Preciso de . . . litros*
Have you distilled water for my battery?	*Tem água destilada para a minha bateria?*

Check the tyre pressures — Verifique a pressão nos pneus
The pressure should be . . . in front and . . . at the back — A pressão deve ser . . . à frente e . . . atrás
Is there a breakdown service? — Há serviço de reparações?
I have had a breakdown (puncture) — Tenho uma avaria (furo)
Where can I find a mechanic? — Onde posso encontrar um mecânico?
Do you do repairs? — Fazem reparações?
I have broken . . . — Parti-quebrei . . .
This does not work — Isto não funciona
Can you do it immediately? — Pode fazer já?
How long must I wait? — Quanto tempo tenho de esperar?
Where can I park? — Onde posso estacionar?
I want to hire a car — Quero alugar um automóvel
How much an hour (a day)? — Quanto por hora (dia)?
Is there an English-speaking driver? — Há um chauffeur que fale inglês?
Go more quickly — Vá mais depressa
Do not drive so fast — Não vá tão depressa
Wait here (over there) — Espere aquí (ali)
Pick me up at . . . — Venha buscar-me às . . .
I must go back by . . . — Tenho de voltar antes das . . . horas

back axle	o eixo traseiro
bend	a curva
boot	o porta bagagens
brake	o travão
breakdown	a avaria
breakdown truck	o carro de socorro
can	a lata
car	o automóvel, o carro
car licence	a licença
caravan	a roulotte
clutch	a embraiagem
convertible	o carro descapotável
cross-roads	a encruzilhada
danger	perigo
distilled water	água destilada
drive, to	guiar, conduzir
driver	o motorista, chauffeur
driving licence	a carta de conduçao
exhaust	tubo de escape
garage	a garagem
gear box	a caixa de velocidades
gear lever	a alavança de mudanças
ignition key	a chave de ignição
jack	o macaco
lever	a alavança
lights	as luzes de tráfego
lubrication	a lubrificação
mechanic	o mecânico
motorway	a auto-estrada
narrow road	a estrada estreita
no entry	entrada proíbida
no parking	estacionamento proíbido
oil	o óleo
overtaking prohibited	proíbido ultrapassar
parking	estacionamento
pedestrian crossing	a passagem de peões
petrol	a gasolina
petrol pump	a bomba de gasolina
radiator	o radiador
repairs	as reparações
reverse	a marcha-atrás
road blocked	estrada obstruída
road junction	cruzamento
roadworks	obras
roundabout	a rotunda
school	a escola
screw	o parafuso
screwdriver	a chave de parafusos
skid	o cruzamento
slippery surface	a superfície escorregadia
slow down	disminuir a velocidade
spanner	a chave de porcas
speed	a velocidade
speed limit	o limite de velocidade

steep hill	*colina escarpada*		two-stroke mixture	*a mistura*
steering wheel	*o volante*		uneven road	*estrada em mau estado*
tank	*o depósito*			
traffic lights	*os sinais luminosos*		unscrew	*desaparafusar*
tyre	*o pneu*		wheel	*a roda*
tyre (tubeless)	*o pneu sem cãmara de ar*			

Numbers

1	*um*	16	*dezesseis*	52	*cinqüenta e dois*
2	*dois*	17	*dezessete*	60	*sessenta*
3	*três*	18	*dezoito*	61	*sessenta e um*
4	*quatro*	19	*dezenove*	62	*sessenta e dois*
5	*cinco*	20	*vinte*	70	*setenta*
6	*seis*	21	*vinte e um*	71	*setenta e um*
7	*sete*	22	*vinte e dois*	72	*setenta e dois*
8	*oito*	30	*trinta*	80	*oitenta*
9	*nove*	31	*trinta e um*	81	*oitenta e um*
10	*dez*	32	*trinta e dois*	82	*oitenta e dois*
11	*onze*	40	*quarenta*	90	*noventa*
12	*doze*	41	*quarenta e um*	91	*noventa e um*
13	*treze*	42	*quarenta e dois*	92	*noventa e dois*
14	*quatorze*	50	*cinqüenta*	100	*cento*
15	*quinze*	51	*cinqüenta e um*		

Photography

I want a black and white (colour) film for this camera	*Quero um filme branco e prêto (em côr) para esta máquina*
Have you any fast film?	*Tem filme rápido?*
Will you load my camera?	*Faça o favor de carregar a máquina?*
Will you develop and print this film?	*Faça o favor de revelar e imprimir este filme?*
I want one (two, three, etc.) print(s) of each	*Quero um (dois, três) positivo(s) de cada*
When will they be ready?	*Quando estarão prontos?*
I must have them by . . .	*Quero-os antes do dia . . .*

camera	*a máquina fotográfica*		filter	*o filtro*
			lens	*a lente*
cine camera	*a máquina cine*		lens-hood	*a protecção da lente*
colour	*a côr*			
develop, to	*revelar*		negative	*o negativo*
enlargement	*a ampliação*		print	*o positivo*
exposure meter	*o fotómetro*		range-finder	*o telémetro*
film	*o filme*		shutter	*o obturador*
film winder	*o passador de filme*		view-finder	*o visor*

Post Office

Where is the nearest post office?	*Onde é Correio mais próximo?*
Give me a stamp(s) for this (these) letter(s)	*Dê-me selo(s) para esta (estas) carta(s)*
I want to express this letter	*Quero mandar esta carta expressa*
I want to register this letter	*Quero registar esta carta*
I want to send this parcel	*Quero mandar este pacote*
Have you any letters poste restante for me?	*Tem alguma carta posta restante para mim?*

I want to send a telegram to . . .	*Quero mandar uma telegrama para . . .*
What is the charge per word?	*Quanto custa cada palavra?*
I want a telephone call to England	*Quero telefonar para Inglaterra*
Will you get me this number?	*Faça o favor de obter-me este número?*
How much will it be?	*Quanto custará?*
You gave me the wrong number	*Deu-me um número errado*

call	*a chamada*	post card	*o postal*
collection	*colecção*	post office	*o correio*
directory	*a lista telefónica*	postal order	*o vale postal*
international money order	*o vale postal internacional*	postman	*o carteiro*
letter	*a carta*	register, to	*registar*
letter box	*a caixa postal*	reply	*responder*
number	*o número*	stamp	*o selo*
paid	*pago*	telegram	*a telegrama*
parcel	*o embrulho*	telephone	*o telefone*

Public Notices

closed	*fechado*	open	*aberto*
cross	*atravesse*	pull	*puxe*
engaged	*ocupado*	push	*empurre*
gentlemen	*homens*	ring	*toque*
information	*informações*	stop, to	*parar*
knock	*bater*	toilet	*toìlette*
ladies	*senhoras*	vacant	*livre*
no entry	*passagem proíbida*	wait	*espere*
		way in	*entrada*
no smoking	*e proíbido fumar*	way out	*saída*
occupied	*ocupado*		

Shopping

Where can I find a . . .?	*Onde posso encontrar um . . .?*
How much is . . .?	*Quanto custa . . .?*
I want to buy . . .	*Quero comprar . . .?*
Have you anything cheaper?	*Tem alguma coisa mais barata?*
I want something like this (that)	*Quero uma coisa igual a esta*
I want more (less) than that	*Quero mais (menos) do que isso*
I will buy this	*Fico com isto*
That's all	*É tudo*
It doesn't fit me	*Não me serve*
It doesn't work	*Não funciona*
Can you change it?	*Pode trocá-lo?*
Will you change it later?	*Poderá ser trocado?*
Can you refund my money?	*Pode devolver o meu dinheiro?*
My English size is . . .	*O meu tamanho inglês é . . .*
Will you measure me?	*Quer tirar-me a medida?*
May I try this on?	*Posso provar isto?*
Can I order one (some)?	*Posso encomendar um (alguns)?*
Send it to this address	*Envie a esta morada*
I will return later	*Voltarei logo*
It is too large (small)	*É demasiadamente grande (pequeno)*
How much each (per kilo, etc.)?	*Quanto é cada (por kilo)?*
Are these ripe (fresh)?	*Estes são maduros (frescos)?*

Repairs

I have broken (torn) this	*Parti (rasguei) isto*
Can you repair it?	*Pode remendá-lo?*
When will it be ready?	*Quando é que está pronto?*
I have to leave by . . .	*Tenho de partir antes do . . .*

Hairdressing

I want a haircut	*Quero um corte de cabelo*
I want my hair trimmed	*Quero que aparem o meu cabelo*
Don't cut it too short	*Não o corte demasiado*
I don't want any oil on my hair	*Não quero brilhantinas no cabelo*
I want a shave	*Quero barbear-me*
Trim my moustache (beard)	*Apare o meu bigode (a minha barba)*
I want this style (show design)	*Quero este estilo*
I want a shampoo and set	*Quero lavar e fazer mise*
I want a permanent wave	*Quero uma permanente*
I want a bleach (colour rinse, tint)	*Quero um descorante (uma tinta, um matiz)*
I want a manicure (pedicure)	*Quero uma manicura (pedicura)*
I want a face massage	*Quero uma massagem na cara*
Thank you. That's very nice	*Obrigado. Está muito bem*
Could I make an appointment for . . . o'clock?	*Posso vir às . . . horas?*

antiques	*antiguidades*	coffee	*o café*
bag	*a carteira*	collar	*o colarinho*
baker	*o padeiro*	comb	*o pente*
ball point	*a caneta esferográfiça*	colour rinse	*a tinta de cabelo*
bathing suit	*o fato de banho*	cotton	*o algodão*
bath salts	*os sais de banho*	cosmetics	*os cosméticos*
battery	*a bateria*	cushion	*a almofada*
belt	*o cinto*	cuff-links	*os botões de punho*
better	*melhor*	cup	*a chávena*
blouse	*a blusa*	dark	*escuro*
book	*o livro*	darker	*mais escuro*
bookseller	*o livreiro*	delicatessen	*mercearia fina*
bracelet	*a pulseira*	department store	*o armazém*
braces	*os suspensórios*		
brassiere	*o soutien*	dictionary	*o dicionário*
brooch	*o broche*	disinfectant	*o desinfectante*
brush	*a escova*	doll	*a boneca*
butcher	*o carniceiro*	draper	*o vendedor de tecidos*
button	*o botão*		
camera	*a máquina fotográfica*	dress	*o vestido*
cardigan	*a camisola*	dry-cleaner	*a tinturaria*
cheap	*barato*	ear-rings	*os brincos*
cheaper	*mais barato*	elastic	*o elástico*
chemist	*o farmacéutico*	envelope	*o envelope*
chiropodist	*o quiropodista*	expensive	*caro*
cigar	*o charuto*	fancy leather goods	*os artipos de fantasia em cabedal*
cigarette lighter	*o isqueiro*		
cleaner	*a tinturaria*	face-powder	*o pó de arroz*
clock	*o relógio*	fine	*fino*
clothes	*a roupa*	finer	*mais fino*
coat	*o casaco*	fishmonger	*o peixeiro*

florist	a florista
fork	o garfo
fur	as peles
glasses	os óculos
gloves	as luvas
gold	ouro
gramophone record	o disco
greengrocer	A loja da fruta e hortaliças
grocer	o merceeiro
guide book	o guia
handbag	a carteira
hat	o chapéu
heavy	pesado
heavier	mais pesado
heel	o salto
high	alto
ink	a tinta
invisible mending	a cerzir
ironmonger	a loja de ferragens
jacket	a casaco curto
jeweller	o joalheiro
label	a etiqueta
large	grande
larger	maior
laundry	a lavandaria
leather	o cabedal
light	leve
lighter (weight)	mais leve
lighter (colour)	mais claro
lighter flint	a pedra de isqueiro
lipstick	o batom de lábios
long	comprido
longer	mais comprido
loose	solto
looser	mais solto
low	baixo
magazine	a revista
manicure	a manicura
map	o mapa
matches	os fósforos
material	o tecido
nail	a unha
nail-brush	a escova de unhas
nail-file	a lima de unhas
narrow	estreita
narrower	mais estreita
necklace	o colar
needle	a agulha
newsagent	o quiosque
newspaper	o jornal
nightdress	a camisa de noite
nylons	as meias de nylon
pale	pálido
pants	as cuecas
panties	as calças
pen	a caneta
pencil	o lápis
perfume	o perfume
photographer	o fotógrafo
pin (safety)	o alfinete de segurança
pipe	o cachimbo
plate	o prato
powder	o pó
powder compact	a caixa de pó
powder-puff	a borla
purse	o porta moedas
pyjamas	os pijamas
radio	o radio
raincoat	o impermeável
razor	a navalha
razor blade	a lâmina de barba
refill	a carga
ribbon	a cinta
rollers	os rolos
sandals	as sandálias
(rope soled)	as alparcatas
saucer	o pires
scarf	o lenço
scissors	a tesoura
shampoo	o shampoo
shaving cream	o creme de barbear
shaving soap	o sabão de barbear
shawl	o chaile
shirt	a camisa
shoes	os sapatos
shoe-laces	os atacadores
shop	a loja
shop assistant	o assistente
short	curto
shorter	mais curto
shorts	calças
silk	a sêda
silver	a prata
size	o tamanho
skirt	a saia
slip	a combinação
slippers	as chinelas
small	pequeno
smaller	mais pequeno
soap	o sabonete
socks	as meias
spectacles	os óculos
stationer	a papelaria
stockings	as meias
strap	a correia
string	o cordel
strong	forte
stronger	mais forte
suede	a pele de antilope

suit	o fato	tighter	mais apertado
suitcase	a mala	tobacco	o tabaco
sun-lotion	o creme de sol	tobacconist	o tabaqueiro
spoon	a colher	toothbrush	a escova de dentes
sun-glasses	os óculos de sol		
suntan cream (oil)	o creme de bronzear	tooth paste	a pasta dentifrícia
		toy	um brinquedo
sweater	a camisola	trousers	as calças
sweets	os doces	umbrella	o guardachuva
tailor	o alfaiate	underwear	a roupa interior
tea	o chá	vacuum flask	a garrafa termos
tie	a gravata	wallet	a carteira
tin	a lata	watch	o relógio
thick	grosso	wide	largo
thicker	mais grosso	wider	mais largo
thin	magro	wine	o vinho
thread	o fio	writing-paper	o papel
tight	apertado	zip	o fecho de correr

Sightseeing

What is there of interest to see?	O que há de interessante para ver?
Is there a tourist information bureau here?	Há aqui um centro de informaçoes?
Is there an English-speaking guide?	Há um guia que fale inglês?
I don't want a guide	Não quero guia
I want to go to . . .	Quero ir a . . .
How much is this excursion?	Quanto é esta excursão?
Are there any boat trips?	Há excursões de barco?
How long does it take?	Quanto. tempo dura?
What time does the trip begin?	A que horas começa a excursão?
When do I get back?	Quando estarei de volta?
We want to be together	Queremos estar juntos
Can I go in?	Posso entrar?
Is this the way to . . .?	É este o caminho para . . .?
How far is it from here to . . .?	A que distância fica daqui?
How long will it take?	Quanto tempo levará?
I want a quick look around the town	Quero fazer uma visita rápida à cidade
This (that) way	Por aqui (ali)
I am lost	Estou perdido

archaeology	a arqueologia	garden (botanical)	o jardim (botânico)
battlement	a ameia		
bridge	a ponte	garden (zoological)	o jardim (zoológico)
building	o edifício		
cable car	o teleférico	gate	o portão
castle	o castelo	gorge	o desfiladeiro
cathedral	a catedral	guide	o guia
church	a igreja	gulf	o golfo
city	a cidade	interpreter	o intérprete
coast	a costa	lake	o lago
excursion	a excursão	law courts	os tribunais de justiça
fountain	a fonte		
gallery (art)	a exposição (de quadros)	lighthouse	o farol
		monument	o monumento
gallery (museum)	o museu	mountain	a montanha
		mountain railway	o cabo teleférico

pottery	*a cerâmica*	street	*a rua*
rest, to	*descansar*	town hall	*a câmara municipal*
river	*o rio*		
ruins	*as ruínas*	valley	*o vale*
seat	*o banco*	village	*a aldeia*
square	*a praça*		

Sport

Do you play . . .?	*Joga . . .?*
May I join you?	*Posso tomar parte?*
Would you like to join in?	*Gostaria de tomar parte?*
Would you like a game of . . .?	*Quer jogar . . .?*
Well played!	*Bem jogado!*
Where is the swimming pool?	*Onde está a piscina?*
Can I hire a bathing costume and/or towel?	*Posso alugar um fato de banho e/ou uma toalha?*
Where are the tennis courts?	*Onde são os campos de tenis?*
Is there a golf course?	*Há um campo de golfe?*
Where can I fish?	*Onde posso pescar?*
I would like to water-ski	*Quero fazer esqui aquático*
What is the cost per tow?	*Quanto custa cada reboque?*
Can I have a motor boat?	*Posso alugar uma lancha?*
Can I launch a boat here?	*Posso lançar um barco aquí?*
I should like to hire a sailing boat	*Quero alugar um veleiro*
Where can I moor?	*Onde posso atracar?*
Can I hire the necessary equipment?	*Posso alugar o equipamento necessário?*
Where can I go horse riding?	*Onde posso montar a cavalo?*
Where (when) can I see horse racing?	*Onde (quando) posso ver corridas de cavalos?*
I want to climb the . . .	*Quero trepar o . . .*
Where can I find a guide?	*Onde posso encontrar um guia?*
What is the weather forecast?	*Qual é a previsão do tempo?*
I am only a beginner	*Eu sou um principiante*
Where (when) can I see a football match?	*Onde (quando) posso ver uma partida de futebol?*
What is the score?	*Qual é o resultado*

athletics	*o atletismo*	caddie	*o caddie*
billiards	*os bilhares*	golf club	*o taco*
boxing	*o pugilismo*	golf course	*o campo de golfe*
bowls	*as bolas*	green	*o relvado*
cycling	*o ciclismo*	hole	*o buraco pequeno*
darts	*os dardos*	miniature golf	*o mini-golfe*
football	*o futebol*	putt	*o putt*
fishing		**horse racing**	
bait	*a isca*	bet	*a aposta*
bait tin	*a lata de isco*	flat race	*a corrida plana*
fishing reel	*a bobina*	grandstand	*a bancada coberta*
fishing rod	*a vara*		
float	*a bóia*	horse	*o cavalo*
hook	*o anzol*	jockey	*o jóquei*
line	*a corda*	steeplechase	*a corrida de obstáculos*
spool	*o carreto*		
golf		tote	*o totalizador*
ball	*a bola*	**horse riding**	
bunker	*o buraco*	horse	*o cavalo*

jump	*o salto*		skis	*os esquis*
pony trekking	*montar num ponéi*		tow-rope	*a sirga*
rein	*a rédea*		**swimming**	
ride	*o passeio*		bathing costume	*o fato de banho*
saddle	*a sela*		dive	*mergulhar-se*
stirrup	*o estribo*		swim	*nadar*
sailing			swimming pool	*a piscina*
anchor	*a âncora*		**tennis**	
helm	*o leme*		balls	*as bolas*
lifejacket	*o cinto de salvação*		doubles	*a partida de pares*
			partner	*o parceiro*
mast	*o mastro*		player	*o jogador*
sails	*as velas*		racquet	*a raqueta*
water ski-ing			service	*o serviço*
water ski, to	*fazer esqui aquático*		singles	*jogo de singulares*
			tennis court	*o campo de ténis*
motor boat	*a lancha*			

Tipping

Is the service included?	*Está incluído o serviço?*
Keep the change	*Fique com o troco*
Tip	*A gorjeta*

Travel

Train/Bus

Can you help me with my luggage?	*Pode ajudar-me com a minha bagagem?*
I shall take this myself	*Eu levarei isto*
Don't leave this	*Não deixe isto*
Where is the . . .?	*Onde está o . . .?*
What is the fare to . . .?	*Qual é preço para . . .?*
Give me a first- (second-) class ticket for . . .	*Dê-me um bilhete de primeira (segunda) classe para . . .*
I want a sleeping-berth	*Quero um beliche (uma cama)*
I want to reserve a seat	*Quero reservar um lugar*
What time is the next (last) train for . . .?	*A que horas sai o último comboio para . . .?*
From which platform does it leave?	*De que plataforma sai?*
Where is the booking (inquiry) office?	*Onde é a bilheteira (informação)?*
Do you stop at . . .?	*Pára em . . .?*
Must I change for . . .?	*Tenho de mudar de combóio para . . .?*
Is this right for . . .?	*Está bem para . . .?*
Where (when) are the meals served?	*Onde (quando) servem as refeições?*
This seat is reserved	*Este lugar está reservado*
Someone has taken my seat	*Alguém ocupou o meu lugar*
Can you find me another seat?	*Pode encontrar-me outro lugar?*
Is this seat vacant?	*Está livre este lugar?*
This seat is (not) vacant	*Este lugar (não) está livre*
May I open (close) the window?	*Posso abrir (fechar) esta janela?*
Where is the toilet?	*Onde está a toilette?*
Where are we?	*Onde estamos?*
I want to put my luggage in the left luggage office	*Quero deixar a minha bagagem no depósito de bagagens*

How much do I owe you?   *Quanto devo?*
Taxi hire
Is there a taxi?   *Há por aqui um taxi?*
I am going to . . .   *Vou para . . .*
Here is the address   *Aquí está o endereço*
I am in a hurry   *Estou com pressa*
Will you drive as quickly as possible   *Faça o favor de guiar o mais rápido possível*
Go more slowly   *Vá mais devagar*

airline office	*os escritórios da linha aérea*
airport	*o aeroporto*
arrival	*a chegada*
bag	*a mala*
berth	*a cama*
blanket	*o cobertor*
boat	*o barco*
booking-office	*a bilheteira*
bus	*o autocarro*
carriage (coach)	*a carruagem*
coach	*o autocarro*
compartment	*o compartimento*
communication cord	*o alarme*
connection	*a ligação*
Customs	*a alfandêga*
Customs officer	*o empregado alfandegário*
departure	*a partida*
dining-car	*o vagão-restaurante*
door	*a porta*
driver	*o condutor/motorista*
entrance	*a entrada*
exit	*a saida*
fare	*o preço da viagem*
half-fare	*meio-bilhete*
inquiry office	*as informações*
journey	*a viagem*
label	*a etiqueta*
last	*último*
luggage	*a bagagem*
luggage-van	*o vagão de bagagem*
next	*próximo*
number	*o número*
passenger	*o passageiro*
passport	*o passaporte*
pillow	*a almofada*
platform	*o cais, a plataforma*
platform ticket	*o bilhete de cais (gare)*
port	*o pôrto*
porter	*o bagageiro*
railway	*a via férrea*
seat	*o lugar*
seat reservation	*a reserva de lugar*
smoking compartment	*o compartimento onde é permitido fumar*
station	*a estação*
station-master	*o chefe de estação*
stop	*a paragem*
subway	*o subterrâneo*
suitcase	*a mala*
taxi	*o táxi*
ticket, single (return)	*o bilhete, simples (de ida e volta)*
tickets, book of	*o caderno de bilhetes*
time-table	*o horário*
train	*o combóio*
tram	*o carro eléctrico*
trunk	*a mala*
waiting-room	*a sala de espera*
window	*a janela*